ALASKAN CRUDE

It's Not About The Oil

Charlie L. Bower III
Sitka, Alaska

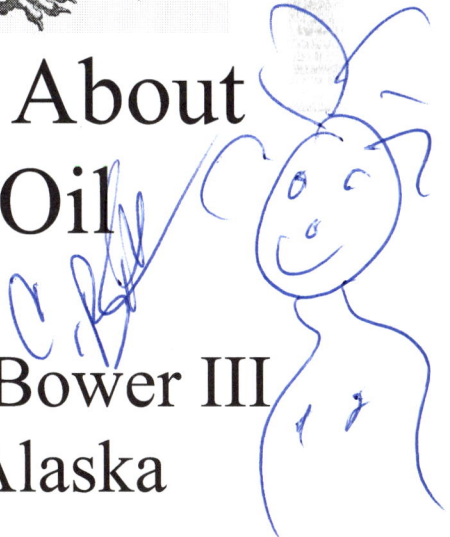

09-03-2011

Cover illustration is GRIDWORK,
a wood engraving by Rebecca Poulson,
copyright Rebecca Poulson.
www.theoutercoast.com

Second Edition   2011

ISBN – 13:978-1456526764
LCCN - 1456526766

Printed in the United States of America.

Dedication

Steve Little said it best:

Each ocean storm eventually ends
so this I dedicate to all of our friends
who went to the sea for the livelihood that they earned
fought life's last bitter storm but never returned.

Contents

Acknowledgements

Many people along the way have helped these stories come together. I have known kind strangers, old salts, beautiful women, and a couple of thugs, they all made it happen. I can't begin to name them all. Some of them a regaled in these pages, some have names I never knew and some I don't remember. It is a long way from the Florida Coast to the Gulf of Alaska and it has been one hell of a trip.

Special thanks to my book mechanics; Susan Royce who took my wrinkled chicken scratched pages and brought them to a working digital copy. Emily Davis, an amazing village school teacher, she edited the pages and corrected my grammar (somewhat). Mary Magnuson, photographer and jack of all trades for helping with layout and images. Thanks to the poets and photographer friends that contributed to the project.

It is been awhile in the making, more than a few barroom discussions. Thanks to all that helped it come together; I hope they all enjoy the read

1

SEATTLE

Arriving in Seattle was quite shocking. Surrounded by huge buildings, all alone, I was far from home and family. Just after a frazzled five day journey from south Florida on a Greyhound bus, there I stood in my corduroy jacket with fake wool lining, jeans without long johns, cotton socks with dingo boots. Bewildered. Orange, hard framed backpack on. I was getting just what I wanted, to get away, as far away as possible. Shivering, I ducked into some pub near the bus station. I was lucky enough to be able to keep drinking in the bars at 18 because of the date they chose, when they swapped it to 21.

Going on about "Alaska" and looking to get to the Alaska state highway ferry system, a fellow in the seat nearby buys me a beer, sits down by me and says, "You know, the ferry takes four long days to Alaska." We go on bullshitting about me trying to get to Alaska. After awhile and a few more beers, he tells me he's got a sister who can get me a cheap ticket to Alaska, "Can do me a favor, save me all the time of that travel." He wanted me to give him the money, and then he'd come back with the ticket. No way was I falling for that. I imagine another beer or two passed. Finally, I was giving up. "If I can go with you, I'll do it." So he made a call or at least pretended to. "Let's go," he says.

Off we went into some towering building. He went up to the informational director and said something to him. As I watched this, I was becoming more convinced. He came back, asked for the money stating that he was clear to go up to see his sister. So I did, I parted with my money, which was about half of what I had. The guy started to head toward the stairway. I started after him. He turned, said he was the only one able to go in to see his sister, for me to wait in the lobby. He assured me it was cool, that he'd be back with the ticket. He was convincing. I watched my money go up the stairs, never to return in any form. I sat there for several hours 'til the building emptied of all business. I was fucked and fucked good because of my trust. "Oh well," I thought, "It was the rush to get to Alaska." Impatience got me.

Now, on the other side of the continent, I felt small, tiny and sad, eyes puddled with tears. I resorted to the collect call. No matter whom I called for help they all said, "You chose your path, so you walk it, and good luck to you.

Knowing that I was now in a fix, I got my directions and kept my southern mouth shut as much as possible. Somehow I got myself to the ferry terminal. I checked on the prices and times of departure to the closest Alaskan town, Ketchikan. There was truly no choice but to continue on. It would just about break me. Like I said, "I had no choice!" I needed to get up there and get some work. I could take either the COLUMBIA or the MALASPINA - large passenger vessels with a vehicle deck. Each ferry had staterooms, a cafeteria with a dining area, viewing area with lockers, and seats that turned into more of a common area for sleeping, reading, and socializing. Then there was the fairly plush bar. Out on the upper deck near the stern of the boat, there was the solarium. People pitched their tents on deck. There were also outdoor lounge chairs for pretty much camping out.

People were pretty well free to carry on as they wanted to. People circled around at the very stern of the boat smoking reefer and having various alcoholic beverages. There were coolers full of a variety of food, picked up at Pike's Place Market in Seattle. A maze of meats, fish, crustaceans, cheese, vegetables, fruits and a full array of t-shirts, caps and such, something of course I was not aware of. But I was hungry, thirsty and near broke. We were underway to the great State of Alaska. I picked me a spot under the cover of the solarium deck where they also had heat lamps for lighting. It wasn't long before thirst fell upon me.

I headed to the vessel's tavern. Taverns have always been good to me for getting hammered and finding work. So, getting down to my last $100.00, I ordered a beer and started to milk it. The bar had five or six people bellied up to it. I started going on about needing a job. "Anything would do, from selling bibles to hard labor," I replied when asked what I was capable of. "I just need a job." The beers kept whittling my cash flow closer and closer to that last C note. I continued to talk to everyone and anyone of my abilities to do or learn just about anything.

I got up to go piss. When I got back there was one fellow sitting to the left of me and one on my right. The fellow on my right got up and went to the head. While he was gone, the fellow on my left said, "That guy," as he pointed to the guy on my right, "said he might help with getting you some work." I puffed up like some rooster protecting his flock of hens when the weasel comes into the henhouse. On his return from the head, I became nervous and tried to figure out the next words out of my mouth, which had always been hard to predict especially after getting liquored up. I couldn't afford to fuck this up. So, I introduced myself. He said his name was Jack. About that same time, the fellow to my left got up and left. So I said, "Well, Jack, that fellow over there said you might know of some work." Jack ordered us both a couple more beers, telling me, "It's possible." I continued to badger him about work and my travels thus far, as well as my financial situation. Jack finished his beers and asked me to meet him in the cafeteria for coffee and breakfast, of course I accepted. He bid me good night.

I was hungry and headed for the dining area. I got in line, figured I would just get a hamburger. I started looking at the cost of the food - I nearly fell over. It was way too expensive. I think I ended up with a ham and cheese on white bread with a bag of chips out of the cooler. It was in the neighborhood of $10.00. That alone took me to my last $100 - I didn't have to break it, but the next time I had to make a purchase, I would have to use my last Benjamin Franklin.

I awoke in the solarium to a beautiful, crisp morning some-where on our way through Canadian waters. The first stop in Alaska was Ketchikan. It was sunny. The water was flat calm with a feeling about it that just eased my soul. The blue green water led to the shores which led to the wondrous green of forest which in turn led to the snow covered tops of the mountains and on to what seemed like a perfect sky. But I had a coffee date with a man about possible work, so I shucked the thought of beauty and was overcome with the feeling of poverty.

Alaskan Crude

I headed down to the cafeteria area. Jack was already seated. I slid up, said "Good morning." He said, "Looks to me like you could use some coffee and breakfast." I agreed. We got up, got in line. Jack was more than twice my age - maybe even triple my age. He was definitely my elder. He was clean shaven, not real tall - 5'10", fairly stocky gentlemen, wore khakis, typical plain shirt with a small round rim cap with fly fishing lures hanging on it.

Jack ordered his breakfast. I got my coffee and put my order in - eggs, toast and hash browns. That was as cheap as it got for an egg breakfast. No meat. As we edged our way to the cashier, I was definitely thinking of the last Benjamin Franklin my fingers were now fondling, now out of my pocket, and in my hand. Jack looks down at me and says, "Put that back in your pocket, you're going to need it later on."

"That's okay, I can get it."

"Put it back in your pocket, you're going to need it later on."

So I looked at him, then I accepted. We spent awhile with breakfast and coffee and coffee and coffee. There was no sense in being in a hurry on the ferry - you're just cruising along at about maybe 15 knots. So we pumped each other for whatever type of information we were willing to share. For me, it was about what kind of work and where. For him, it was what was going on with me, what was it I might be running from, and how I came to be there. "See you at the bar later?" he asked. I replied, "Sure."

With that morning gone, back to the solarium I went. I got myself joined in with the circle group

at the stern. Me, accustomed to brown weed, Mexican or Columbian, discovered that this was the
shit, the mean green, the bad ass, the ganja. It
wasn't long and I was on one of the deck chairs
watching the world go by. Finally, when I came to
from my trip of green, blue and white ecstasy, I
realized the landscape. I figured it must be time to
wet the whistle.

As I entered the vessel's tavern and gazed
around, my eyes fell on Jack. Jack was sitting at
the bar with a stunning young woman with long
red hair. I went over and bellied up next to Jack,
ordered a beer, and pulled out my Benjamin. Jack
told the bartender he'd get it. He looked at me and
said, "Put it back in your pocket, you're going to
need it later." I didn't want to do battle over the
beer, especially in front of the pretty girl. Next
Jack said, "Charlie, I'd like you to meet my friend
Patty." She was pretty with a bright smile.

The three of us started yakking it up for awhile. They were trying to convince me not to get
off in Ketchikan, to just stay on the boat - no one
would check my ticket. Tickets were hardly ever
checked unless you were boarding through the
ticket purchase area. If you had already purchased
a ticket, you just headed back to the vessel via the
gangplank.

Pretty Patty had to disembark from the
sanctuary of the tavern for one reason or another.
When she stood up it became clear she wasn't just
stunning, she was also sexy. Not heavy, not skin-
ny, beautifully proportioned. She wore a fur coat
over a well-fitted blouse with a skirt that led down
to her tight white net stockings. The thought came

to me that I would pay $5.00 for a shot glass of that girl's bath water.

"Man."

We said we hoped to see her later; she looked right at me and said, "You will if you stay on the ferry and don't get off in Ketchikan." She turned around and walked out. Jack and I finished our beers. He once again asked me to meet him back at the tavern about dinner time. With the breakfast and the beers, and the possibility of work - I was feeling kind of uneasy with his generosity. I did definitely need work. So, I replied, "Yes, maybe I'll see you back here." I thanked him for the beers and headed back up to the solarium.

I gathered up some different clothes to wear. In the head (or re-stroom), there were shower stations in a row. I got cleaned up, went back up, and packed up most of

my things. Arrival was mid to early morning in Ketchikan. I had somehow come under the impression that the first town I came to would have a boom going on. I thought I would see evidence of tents belonging to gold miners or loggers pulling logs down Main Street; dirty hard working men being thrown out in the streets from the taverns; Cancan girls who turned into ladies of the night after the dancing stopped or stood on the second story balconies calling down to the men in the street.

Alaskan Crude

I got myself calmed down and decided to go meet Jack. We weren't there yet and I was getting hungry. I swung back into the tavern - it was beginning to feel like an old hat - comfortable. Most of the drinkers were either in the bar or were topside making their own. Of course, there was Jack and the rest of the regulars that passed the time traveling with a beer instead of a book. So I said my hellos and sat down by Jack. I asked if he was still interested in dinner. He downed his beer and we headed for the cafeteria. Again, as we got to the cashier, I pulled out my hundred. He looked at me again and said, "How many times do I have to tell you - you're going to need it later?" I liked this guy but I was really starting to feel uneasy with him purchasing all the goods. Once again, I let him. I felt like he was maybe trying to purchase me.

While we were eating we were still sort of probing each other. We finished up and he asked if I wanted to grab another beer. That was it - no more would I accept a fucking thing from this man until we cleared the air. I said, "Look, I don't know what your real deal is, but nobody is this nice for free where I come from. So if you think you're going to fuck me or something like that, you're totally wrong." His reaction wasn't violent or rude or even disappointed. He calmly said that he was traveling alone and that it was just nice to have company and bullshit with someone fresh and green to Alaska like myself. We had gotten liquored up and told each other some pretty good stories over the last couple days - at least stories we were willing to reveal. His calm replies gained my trust. He was actually just being honest. I said, "Okay Jack, let's go have one."

While we were having our one, two, three, Jack realized that I was planning on hopping ship in Ketchikan. Still, he kept telling me, suggesting to me, that I hang on and hang out. Once again, we parted ways, me to the solarium and Jack to his stateroom.

Back in the solarium it was night. Against the stern rail stood the silhouette of Patty with her long hair, tight, voluptuous body. Of course I had to go to her. I said "hello" and we started talking. She told me of the other cities yet to come and that there might be a better opportunity in Juneau or Sitka. She tried to convince me to stay on the ferry and to go further. We went on talking for awhile. It got late, we said good night.

Curled up in my sleeping bag thinking of my situation, I fell asleep. I woke to people shoving and stuffing sleeping bags, tents, backpacks, and coolers. Within me rose a quickness to do the same. My fellow travelers were packing up like

someone had just sounded the abandon ship horn.

I headed down to the main deck just to find out we were still over an hour away.

I could have had coffee first, and seeing as to how I didn't, I figured I had better do it second. Who did I see in the cafeteria? Jack. I got a cup and sat down at his table, my pack at my feet. I just had to check it out in Ketchikan. Jack knew there was no sense in trying to talk me out of it. He gave me some last minute advice while I sat there anxiously awaiting my departure. "If you get there and take a look and it's not what you think, try just walking back on and wave your old ticket at the porter. He'll probably think you just went into town for a look about. It takes the ferry system several hours at some stops to get the vehicles off and rearranged with the new ones coming on. There's time to catch a bus or hitchhike to town. Hang out off the ferry for awhile and see the sites."

We arrived at the Ketchikan ferry terminal. We said our goodbyes and I threw the old hard frame on my back. I went below decks, walked off, and stepped on my first Alaskan soil. I went up on the road system, starting hiking into town. As I walked up on the City of Ketchikan, I didn't see the miner's tents or women on balconies. I saw a log truck go by with a load of fresh cut headed somewhere. It basically looked like a regular town; except I did notice there were a shit load of dudes looking pretty much just like me, who had done the same as me - a one-way ticket to Ketchikan. Now, we all wandered the same sidewalks, looking for the same thing. There were only going to be so many jobs; there were definitely more ferries coming carrying more normals, a couple times a week - which caused me to think of Jack and Patty. No gold at my feet, no one seen cutting timber. I started to think about the advice I had been given and how long before the ferry departed. It didn't look as prosperous as I had thought it might in Ketchikan.

Alaskan Crude

I hitched a ride back to the ferry terminal, sucked up a coupled of deep breaths, got my old ticket out, walked down the ramp, flashed my ticket at the porter. He just nodded and up the stairway to the main deck I went. The porter had recognized me from earlier, just like Jack said he would.

Back aboard I went and got re-situated in the solarium. The party was still was going on for those who had more northern destinations. Relieved that I was aboard, I joined in and reaped the benefits of generosity. People were so damn friendly. It felt uncanny, but at the same time, wonderful. Since getting on the ferry, no one had tried to deceive me in any manner.

Leaving Ketchikan, we were back under way. I figured where I might find Jack as well as Patty. I proceeded to the bar knowing that even if my ticket was checked, I wouldn't get kicked off until the next stop, Wrangell. There they both sat talking and smiling. They seemed a bit surprised to see me. I bellied up next to them and said, "I decided to take your advice." Both of them smiled and said "Good." They both were headed to Sitka. Jack had a friend there and Patty a husband to meet. Jack offered me a beer, I accepted. It was kind of like signing adoption papers this time. He wanted someone to travel and hang with along the way. I needed someone to help me out and get a start. From then on, his word was word.

For the next few days I drank and ate on Jack's tab. I told him of my flights from the cocaine train I'd been riding in south Florida, due to having sex with the oldest of three sisters in my neighborhood, which ended with my neck broken in three places courtesy of the guy down the street who had always loved the youngest sister, the sister about my age. Not being able to see through his jealousy and anger, he couldn't understand that I was getting my wings from the oldest sister. Plus, we kept it hidden as much as possible. He confronted me one night, we fought and with one bad judo front throw he landed across my shoulders he snuffed my head under my chest. The bones of C5, C6 and C7 snapped like twigs. The situation resulted in a lawsuit and several months of healing between the hospital and my sister's couch. Once out of the body cast and off the couch, I pursued the settlement. The settlement was made quickly and the bender began immediately. It didn't take me long between the alcohol, cocaine, weed and gambling when I woke up back on my sister's couch sweaty with dirty clothes on. I checked my wallet - I was down to $700.00 from $30,000.00.

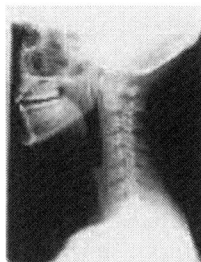

During my healing, I met my brother-in-law's brother who had told me about Alaska. So I figured I better get out while I still could. Alaska was still part of the United States and as far away as I could get from my present state – that was with double meaning.

I went on with stories of the Greyhound trip and my travels. I prodded Jack for information on what type of work his friend did. Jack told me his friend was the surveyor on a road they were widening to the mill in Sitka. If work with Jack's friend wasn't possible, then perhaps I could get on with some electrician friends in Juneau. As the beers, food, and conversation went on, so did the towns; Wrangell, Petersburg, Juneau, Haines, Skagway and then finally Sitka. I never once got off again in fear of my ticket being checked. Sitka - the place of possible prosperity - I was excited.

Jack told me to meet him in the ferry parking lot. He drove a little white Volkswagen hatchback. He picked me up and we immediately drove out towards the mill. The landscape faced the ocean, full of small islands and rock piles. A great volcano, Mt. Edgecumbe, was in the distance with a snow-covered top. We got out to where they were blowing the road to the mill. There were several men going on about their business. Loaders scooped up the loose rock; a couple of men were on top of the ridge driving marker stakes; a fellow shot a transom standing at road level. We pulled over. Jack got out, motioned for me to follow.

Jack introduced me to Frank Brown. Frank looked like the Gnarly Woods Man: long silver beard, mustache and facial hair all bonding together as one, silver hair down near the middle of his back, logger boots with logger pants cut that frizzled a few inches past the top of the boot, leather vest with native embroidery. He wasn't a large man; he was a little big man.

The Sitka mill was a pulp mill that made various paper products such as tissue and writing paper. He said there were no positions available, as he looked at me.

"Meet me at the Pioneer Bar about 5:00," Frank told Jack.

Jack said, "See you there."

I said, "Nice to meet you." Frank looked at me and nodded.

Well, with not much to do, Jack decided we might as well go wait at the Pioneer Bar; that way we'll be there at 5:00. We went ahead and got started a couple of hours early.

I was looking at the hundreds of pictures that hung on the walls of the huge halibut. There were pictures of record size King salmon, seine boats that were choked with herring or salmon, boats that ran aground, boats that were sunk or on fire. There was money tacked all over the ceiling with commercial fishing vessels names written in black marker. The drinks were definitely kicking in. I just started rambling on about who knows what.

Well, Frank showed up, got a drink, and I'm still just going on about the pictures and such. There were a few pictures of humpback whales bubble feeding. Frank and Jack were putting up with me going on about how I've never seen a whale. It wasn't long before my first Cheechako nickname became "The Mouthfrom the South." Anyhow, they listened to me going on about the whales. Frank got up, went through the swinging doors to the liquor store. He came back with a brown sack. Frank looked at me and said, "Let's go." I looked at Frank, Frank looked at me. I looked at Jack because Frank kind of scared me for some reason, something about his looks and his manner - I wasn't sure of. Like I said, Jack's word was word. He told me to go on.

"Where we going?" I asked. Jack said "Go on." I
looked at Frank, got up, and we headed out to the
parking lot and got into his old station wagon.

It was all a mystery. Not knowing what to
expect, we drove over the bridge to Japonski Isl-
and, around the small harbor out to the airport.
Frank pulled up to a chain fence gate, got out and
unlocked it. He got back in and asked me to shut
and lock the gate. In front of me were small single
and double seater Cubs and Cessna planes. Frank
drove over to one of the Cubs. He got the brown
bag out of the wagon, put it into the little Cub, and
directed me to get in the back. My heart rate in-
creased, I looked at Frank, crawled in the back
seat and buckled up – I thought "What the fuck?"

Frank hopped
in, fired up,
did some
checks, put on
his headset,
and called the
tower for
clearance to
take off. We
started rolling
out to the

strip - up and off we went. Awesome!!

He flew me over Sitka Sound, which was
loaded with islands and passages. Out to and over
the top of Mt. Edgecumbe to look down into the
center of the volcano. I had only seen a volcano
on National Geographic or in a book at school.
Then out to the coast of the briny North Pacific
Ocean. Low and behold, a pod of humpback
whales swam below. We flew low, almost low

enough for the blow from the spout to touch the plane. It was my first whale sighting. We circled a few passes. Amazing! Frank headed the plane to the outside coast, flew over a long sandy beach and looked it over. There were logs and more logs. He circled around and went in for a landing. It was bumpy and bouncy. We came to a stop.

Frank unbuckled and opened up, lifted his seat so I could get out - "Grab the beer," he said. This was cooler than shit. We sat on a probably four to five foot round log, and looked out across the surge of the great North Pacific. I popped the top on a Lucky Lager. I was going on thanking Frank when a couple of Sitka blacktail deer popped out of the woods. We talked and drank a couple more beers. Frank said we better get going, so we packed up the empties and crawled back in the cub.

Taking off was a bumpy as landing. Flying back, I filled my eyes with boats, birds, snow-covered mountains full of green, and the blue of the Pacific Ocean. Never had I had such a day. The view of the city came closer and closer. The city stretched along the shores of a great sound, leading straight to the ocean. "Sitka by the Sea." Frank radioed the airport tower and gets clearance to

land. He put down and pulled over to his stall. As we got out I couldn't thank him enough. My mouth was running like a broken toilet valve.

We got back to the Pioneer Bar and Jack was there. I just couldn't shut up, plus Jack was just feeding the drinks to me. Frank said we could flop at his hotel room. The company he worked for paid a room at the Shee Atika, one of the fancier hotels in town. So cool. I figured I'd had a day like no other and got a place to crash.

The next morning, Jack and Frank told me they were going sailing with some lady friends for an overnight. I could use the room but needed to be gone when they got back the following day. I said "Thanks," they said "Goodbye."

Well, I tooled along the harbors and ended up back at the Pioneer. Without Jack, I had to bust out that last Benjamin Franklin. He was right again. I'm sure I was trying to hustle up some work. When to no avail, I headed back to Frank's room. I was kicking it, lying there watching TV when there was a knock on the door. I got up to answer it, opened the door and there stood this dark haired, beautiful dark eyed native woman. She asked about where Frank was. I told her that he would be back tomorrow. She looked at me and said, "You'll do." She kind of pushed her way into the room, shut the door, and dropped her jacket. What was in front of my eyes was all woman. It took me about two seconds to lip lock her. She was coming in to get some - I had no reason to disappoint her. Later on, she just got up, put her shit back on, said thanks, and that she'd see me around. I said good night and shut the door.

Alaskan Crude

When I woke up, I got my stuff together to leave. As I opened the door, I felt the sun was shining on my face. I thought that if this is just the beginning, I could only imagine what the future might bring. I never saw Jack again. Frank would pass our hellos back and forth until Frank told me years later that Jack had passed on. Now Frank is gone. I can't thank either of them enough for my first day in Sitka.

2

CHOICES

In life there are a certain amount of choices that are made for you. You may have either been for or definitely against them. The choice chosen for you, in time, may have some outcome on your personal, physical or mental state of health. Throughout my childhood, I had decisions made for me. Actually, as a child, I suppose you're just living out someone else's uncertain moments with them hoping to find and share those moments of warmth, love and understanding. From the time

20

you're born, you know there is pain. Back in the
day when first born, a baby was held upside down
and smacked on the backside to wake it up, make
it cry and start breathing in the life giving air.
From circumcision to the flu shot, living through
other people's decisions can sometimes be over-
whelming. Prosperous maybe, possibly even
overwhelmingly prosperous, but who knows the
price one has to pay for prosperity that was ob-
tained in and through decisions not truly of your
own choosing. Forced by guilt to continue on some
legacy, or to choose to be the defiant person
swearing to "never be like that." The agony of
growing up against the choices or decisions made
for you could cause one to reflect from his childhood through adulthood. Hopefully they would
see the mistakes made by the parents, elders or
guardians and not become angry from those memories. Rather, finding their life better due to the
capability of being able to make their own choices
and not following in the footsteps of their mentors.
I was angered though, at my parents. God knows
I loved them but I was still angered. They died
early on when I was a child. My mother died when
I was eight. The only real recollection of my mother's death, even though I was eight, was my
youngest sister being pretty much forced to look
after me, while my mother was at work or out on
the town. My sister ran with a group of kids in the
trailer park. My youngest sister being three years
older than myself, having her own problems, had
me as her sidekick. I had problems with her
friends and their rules and expectations. The rule
was basically simple. You either join in so that you

are as guilty as them or you get the shit knocked out of you. Even at age eight, I was forced to join in their trailer park thieving and drug use. I don't know or remember what type of drug I was on the day I found out about my mother's death. I do know that I was spaced out of my mind. I sat in the corner of the empty living room in an abandoned trailer. Suddenly, one of the gang came bursting in, looked right at me and said, "Your mother is dead." Stoned out of my eight-year old mind, I could still comprehend the words from his mouth. I remember running to my mother in bare feet across the unmowed lawn, full of sticker-burrs. But my mother was no longer waiting for me at home. I can't say I recall much after that; just small glances of the burial in the hill country of Texas where she was from. I always felt my parents cared more for their needs than that of my sisters' and mine. They lived a hard life, unable to get along. We were raised with divorce and death. Luckily, I had a sister, 18 years older than me at the time.

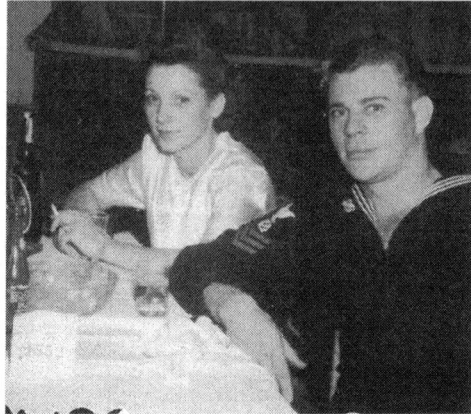

After my mother's passing a decision had to be made. My father was a shrimp boat captain and unable to take proper care of my youngest sister and I. A choice was made to have us go and live in Florida with my oldest sister. It was some start to find out at an early age that life reveals itself moment by moment; I was one who did. Life was like a swift, silent arrow that suddenly pierces your heart. Hopefully the arrow carried the love of comet, not the poison of sadness and sorrow. Losing my mother was shock enough, but now I was moving to a different state. While I was used to relocating, moving from school to school in Texas, this move seemed huge. Sometimes I went from being the brightest kid in class down to the slowest one in class; depending on which school I was transferring to or from.

For the next few years my oldest sister and her husband raised me, with their two daughters, my nieces. Something must have been passed

down through genetics. We were still moving from place to place fairly often; either due to my brother-in-law's work or possibly the needs and choices forced on us by my sister. Whether intentional or not, we four children found life and took life with considerable amount of stress. When one lives under the tension of stress due to money, greed, domestic violence or abuse, that person will have those memories or characteristics to reflect on during their growth to maturity. These ill mannered and inconsiderate actions may travel through generations of time. That was what my parents did, so that's the way we were going to do it, too.

"Children are to be seen not heard." I've heard these types of sayings enough. Couldn't one reflect and possibly change the way your parents were, using the same basic foundation that was passed to you from them? In today's uncertain world, the crimes are unbelievable. The posters on major shopping center store walls attest to this. Not just a small part of the wall, but the larger portion of the wall. Missing women and children. What happened? Where did they disappear? As I think about this, I picture my own children on those posters. It brings the vilest, disgusting thoughts with feelings of the most excruciating pain. Whoever is responsible for bringing such horror into a family life needs to reflect on their soul as well as their mental state of mind. Those trying to figure it out find out and help out, must endure tremendous amounts of pressure. Then to return at the end of the day and be with your own family and moral values.

Values: how much is it worth? What or how much do I get from it? I value you as a friend, lover, postman or grocery clerk. I value my family utmost in the world. Let's trade this for that. One may be small and the other large, due to value. A drink of water in the desert, I would say valuable. Getting a drink of water in a rainforest, not so much so. A mother's love, a father's strong handshake, a loving smile or facial gesture, are things of value. From day to day I believe we like to think of ourselves as valuable; valuable to loved ones and home place. To a parent or person who made good and decent choices towards a valuable future. Perhaps if not family, then perhaps you find value at your work place. There may be an individual that brings a little something extra to his or her surroundings. Sometimes value comes with a price and it can take years to find that price.

Such was the case when my father remarried, then sent to Florida for me. At the time, my youngest but elder sister was out on her own. I moved back to Texas. My father had married a Cuban woman with a daughter. Her daughter was a of couple years younger than I. We lived in a doublewide trailer on an acre of land just outside of town. I tried to settle in; started school. While in Florida, I was allowed to grow my hair long. My father was not the Texas long hair type. Another unsettling choice was made for me. They called it "the boy's hair cut." Feeling the embarrassment of meeting my peers with hair tuned to the Beach Boys' style, I walked into class looking like a sheared sheep. Maybe at such a moment you find the characteristic of humility. Then you have to adjust and find strength. Not realizing that in a few days that if they really were your friends, they still would be. And somewhere, sometime we will each suffer an embarrassment.

So I came home after facing a frustrating day to find my father packing his sea-bag, as I look at this woman I know little about, and knowing my father will be gone for several weeks. It seemed there was going to be a new set of choices and values set. During the school year, my father would come in briefly to sell his catch and regear up. My stepmother, stepsister, and I never became very close but we managed to get along without too much frustration.

In the summer time, my father would pack my sea-bag and we would shove off to sea. Spending weeks on end, dragging for shrimp off the coast of Texas. We worked at night. Three tows or drags a night. I was made to get up for whatever watch, which was also my father's. One of my jobs was to check the tri-net - a small net to help you calculate the size and amount of product going in your nets. On each tow, I would empty the nets on the deck. For a child to see such creatures of the depths was eye popping. Once the nets were shaken and reset, it was time to head the shrimp, always being careful of Moray Eels, sea snakes, poisonous fish and crabs with their pinchers a-pinching.

Once, the three of us, the rig man, header and me, were sitting on our small crate boxes (they keep your ass on the deck but not actually on it). Doing our jobs, we reached in to the edges of the mound of trash fish and shrimp. We picked and headed the shrimp, scrapping to the side of the trash. All of a sudden, the header jumps to his feet, and let out a bellowing scream. We looked over at him and hanging from the center of his crotch was a blue crab.

The crab had crawled up under his ass. The crate the header was sitting on let his nut hang out of his shorts and unbeknownst to all but the blue crab; which was now swinging from one of his nuts. The question was now how to get the already pissed off crab dislodged from his nut sack with the least amount of pain.

We could break its leg off but the clamp of the claw would still remain. It didn't sound good. We could've just pulled it - but that wouldn't work either. Brilliant minds work in brilliant ways. We got a bucket of seawater. The header swatted his nut sack with the attached crab into the bucket. Once the crab was comfortable again, it simply let go.

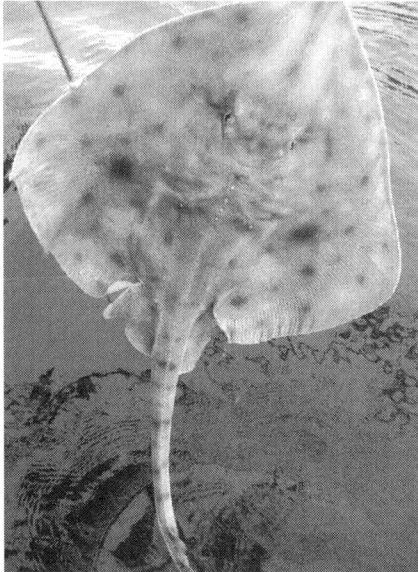

Sometimes we would have sharks trailing the vessel, waiting for us to pick the tow bags so they could try to rip through to the bounty. Occasionally we would pick up a large shark or string ray. We would kill it and use it as a wench to swing it over the rail and cut it free. My father believed in working me like a man. He also paid me like one. Not as an adult man but still as a young man. Not too much slack was given. I was paid the sell-able fish money. In the mornings after the last haul and all the work was done, I would save a few squid. With a shark hook and line, I would slap chain in the water making the sound of unsellable product being tossed over. This always attracted fish of all species to the surface. I would then toss my baited hook right in front of the fish I wanted. I mostly targeted Cobia. My only problem turned out to be greed - I was catching fish larger than I could get aboard. Instead of asking my father, I would usually get one of the crewmen up to help me get the fish over the rail. I knew my father would be angry if I disturbed his sleep. After a few times waking whoever up, I was instructed to only catch fish I could deal with on my own.

After a couple of summers of this, I started longing for some summer in town with my friends. That never happened. What did happen was that my father passed away. My father died of emphysema - he chain-smoked unfiltered cigarettes and pounded down black coffee, a "fisherman's folly." For years I watched him spit or vomit up blood. He ended up in the big city hospital just to catch pneumonia from his roommate. That finished him off. I was never allowed to visit my father while he was in the hospital.   I suspect he didn't want me to see him at his weakest. Lord knows I wished I could have been there to hold his loving, strong hand. One of my most unforgettable memories was his funeral when seeing my father in his casket. When someone you love is dying, you do all you can to be with them, for that chance will never come again.

I must have suppressed a lot of my early childhood. Although I can remember some things, a lot of things are not clear and appear as small, broken pieces like flash cards or a movie on DVD that skips around. Never being able to collect

enough information to confirm the story. It leaves you always wondering. As with quite a few things, I found value with the passage of time. After spending years of being angry with my parents and with God for taking them so early in my life, I know the value of those summer fishing trips with my father. We shared a workload together, working the rigging or eating at the galley table and doing what I was told by a direct, firm, but still loving voice. In time I forgave my parents and God. It certainly wasn't over night.

Another leg of my life was about to unfold. Now that my father had died, the family started to argue over where my place should be. My uncle and aunt thought I should be with them and their children. My oldest sister was willing to fight tooth and nail and not just for me, but for family belongings as well. Finally my uncle pulled me aside and asked me "man to man" where I wanted to live. The choice was unbelievably mine, and so I chose. I chose to go back to Florida with my oldest sister. I knew I would be near my youngest sister, who had always been there for me any time she could. As a result of all the things that happened to me by age 11, I must have been some kind of messed up kid. In addition to losing my parents, my grandparents were getting old and near to passing on. It's said that no parent should have to see their children die. Unfortunately this happened on both sides of my family. I envy people who have a clear vision of their childhood and hope that they have loving and caring memories. I know there is enough bad out there that no one male, female, child, adult or elderly person needs to experience.

Back to Florida I went. My oldest sister was into horse showing, the breaking and breeding business; that meant we were all in the business. Cleaning stalls, feeding, grooming and going to horse shows became a way of life. Winning a competition event, such as roping cattle or barrel racing, made a horse more valuable. These two events were most often done with the quarter horse breed. A thoroughbred may be entered into an English pleasure event. I assure you, it may be pleasure for the person riding the horse, but behind the scenes there is a lot of work happening. Tension in the family was never ending. My brother-in-law worked his regular job and then came home to build a horse walker (a contraption used to walk four horses at a time in a circle). He did this all the while building a house, barn and fencing in the property. Basically, we were trying to keep up with the Joneses, as the old saying goes, or with my sister's never ending need for more. It finally became unbearable. My sister and brother-in-law got divorced. Losing my brother-in-law was a lot like losing my father. Even though I know I was my father's son, I was around my brother-in-law enough to be imprinted somewhat by him. My brother-in-law instilled values in me that I carry with me to this day.

Moving to a little cow town that also produced quite a bit of vegetables, my sister opened up a ladies boutique in a town that was pretty much all Levi or Wrangler jeans. She started another failing business. Of course, her two daughters and I started school. I went into the work program, only taking basic courses. At lunch time my boss, a coarse sun-soaked man, skin tough and dry, a mason or block layer by trade, hardened by time spent in prison, taught me how to set up the 35 pound cinder blocks, mix the mortar. All in all I became a mason's tender. When there was no work in construction, I would head to the fields to pick vegetables or load watermelon trucks. People who purchased watermelons in the produce department of their favorite market more than likely

31

had no idea the amount of sweat it took to get that melon to market.

I also believe my oldest niece enrolled in the work program, working for my sister, her mother. Never being paid proper wages, she was allowed to rummage through the clothes shop and at least be one of the most fashionable dressed young ladies in town. My youngest sister had married a man who I barely recall now. They lived just off a beautiful Florida river that we sometimes go to for a long day of canoeing. We would stop to sift for shark teeth in the shallows of the river. At one time the land and river were covered by ocean. Some of the creatures got land locked and died there, leaving their remains to be filtered out many years later. There were lazy alligators sunning on the banks. We were always aware of water moccasins, especially while swimming. If we camped and stayed over night on the river, I would set a trout line out for catfish. That river held some of my better memories from that time. I'm glad now and then that we made the choices to spend time together doing these things.

Well, as time went on, my sister's ladies boutique did indeed fail. It was a good idea in a town that was not ready for it. The town was a "good old boys" town with traits and traditions passed down that were not to be changed easily. Once again we moved back to the east, or gold coast, of Florida. We moved into a large trailer park that had a clubhouse, pool, tennis courts and racket ball courts. I must have been 16 by then. I remember tying to get my sister to take me to the Department of Motor Vehicles for my driver's license. She wouldn't take me; instead she let me drive her red

Sting Ray Corvette to the Department of Motor Vehicles without a license. No one asked how I got
there, just if I had a vehicle to take the driving part
of the test. We proceeded and I passed the test.

In the trailer park I soon met some other
kids, particularly three brothers. Being in a big city
and old enough to be rebellious, "I" became a
"we." We faced some of life choices as a group.
Instead of having a decision made for us, we would
take it upon ourselves to rule our lives. The oldest
brother was strong and reasonable, but still not
afraid to take a chance. He always stood his
ground. The middle-aged brother was always pay-
ing attention to the truth and reality of a situation.
The third and youngest brother was thin and wiry
and ran more to the wild side. There was one other fellow besides me, a fairly large fellow with an
acne problem who lived at home with his mother.
He was more of the worrywart of the crowd. He
eventually brought the inevitable. He was the
weak link so to speak, breaking a chain that
needed to be broken.

Sometimes things need to be let go. The
boys' mother was quite a woman to raise not only
the boys, but two daughters as well. They accepted me as part of the family until they fought
amongst themselves. People don't want to get in a
family blood battle unless it's with their own blood.
We got into smoking marijuana and drinking or
doing about anything we could get our hands on.
We didn't know it at the time, but we were about
to share in decision making amongst ourselves. In
time, these would be memories of the past that
would last a lifetime. We didn't look to the future.

Alaskan Crude

We were just trying to survive in the present. We were just teenagers testing each other for position and status that seemed to get worked out in a slap box fight or wrestling match. Over time we seemed to figure out who was the strongest, smartest or just plain craziest.

I was still going to school and living under the rules of my sister, who was busy with opening another "ladies boutique" with the merchandise left from the previous shop. I'm sure somehow or the other I would have made it without her. Still, I could never be more grateful for her. Though I spent many years being unforgiving, I appreciated the sacrifices she made for my youngest sister and me. Her daughters may have had a little more consideration from her through life. There always was love in the bowl; the helpings just never got dealt out in large amounts.

I remember when we were raising horses. I had received a Welch pony the Christmas before. Though we lived in the country, a lot of the kids were riding little 100 hp motorcycles. I was conti-nuously saying how I would like to sell my horse and trade it for a small motorcycle.   When Christ-mas morning came, out in the yard under the big pine tree, what to my surprise did I see? There sat a Huffy 10-speed bicycle. I surely was willing to trade one type of mobile transportation for anoth-er, just not one powered by me! Plus, I did favor my pony. I felt cheated and demoralized. She sold the pony, bought something cheaper without regard for my wishes.

When there is a never-ending need for one's self, there just isn't enough room in one's soul or spirit for anything else. Someone or something may someday come along and bite you in the ass. Maybe that's karma. In time my sister would feel the effects of her actions.

Back at the trailer park, we three band of brothers started to hang tight together. While never doing anything bad enough for the cops to catch us, we were at the same time put on the suspect list for petty crimes throughout the trailer park or surrounding area. We mostly skipped school and hung out over at our buddy's house while his mother was at work. We smoked pot and drank whatever we could find. It helped, or so we thought at the time, that his mother was an alcoholic.

It's not like we didn't work. I mowed grass or whatever work I could find in the trailer park. We were always on the look out for cans or returnable pop bottles. Car batteries could be traded for $5.00 to $7.00 a piece.   We stripped radiators of copper, and scrapped aluminum. All in all, we were trying to get by, to get high and to eat. Usually, at the end of the week we would gather up our saleable treasurers and head out for the recycle center, otherwise known as the junkyard. After the junkyard man shrewdly weighed the various metals and counted the batteries, we would get our money. Of course he didn't care where the stuff came from. The cops were at the junkyards as much as the donut shops. We also needed to stop at one of the local quick marts to sell soda bottles to get enough gas to get out the road to the junkyard.

Alaskan Crude

Drinking age for alcohol was 18 so it was usually pretty easy to get someone to buy for us - if we were lucky enough to have located that many pop bottles and recyclables. Of course for a little side income to keep the little happy sack happy or re-supplied, I would sometimes sell joints or marijuana cigarettes in school or outside of school. By that time I had made acquaintances that were glad to front me the weed, in turn I was helping them get rid of it. A win-win situation, I thought. Later I found that if I didn't sell enough, I was certain to use it up amongst the guys and myself. Putting me into debt. Always playing catch up. Some things never seem to change in life. I've been playing catch up ever since, or possibly before I even realized it.

The three brothers and I were friends for a while. I suppose a year or so. It was sort of a ruling around the trailer park. Sometimes we would get the use of a vehicle, cruise the beaches or gather up the fishing rods and we would head to one of the jetties or piers to fish. I don't recall ever catching much more than a buzz or a hang over. We pretty much used fishing as a way to get the car to cruise for chicks, beer, whiskey or drugs. It was not an uncommon thing to do on a southern Florida night. It was always either a clear starry night with a mild breeze that kept the bugs down or there were large buttermilk clouds that seemed to consume the sky, holding out the brightness of the moon like a frosted lampshade would keep out the glare of the flame.

I once saw a rock concert, one of the many from that time in my past. We traveled up state into central Florida to Tampa Bay stadium to see

Alaskan Crude

Led Zeppelin (this was 1977). The sky was clear,
the day hot and humid as we started our trip. As
we drove we ran into broken rain showers. On the
concert ticket it said "rain or shine." With 80,000
people, the band came on. By the second song
everybody was rockin', tripin', dancing or singing.
Like night takes over dark, there in the distance
the blackest rain and lighting cloud ever with sunshine 360 degrees around it, traveled towards the
stadium like metal to a magnet. First to see it,
then to feel the vibration of the rumble of thunder
with the adjacent snap of lightening, as the dark
cloud approached, the rain hit. Yes, it started with
a drop, but within seconds it developed into a torrential downpour. The tarps the musicians played
under quickly loaded up with water. They ripped
and dumped. Unable to continue safely, they
called off the concert.

    This all took place in just a matter of mo-
ments.   80,000 pissed off ready to party "rain or
shine" fans were told to exit in an orderly manner.
Guess what? No can do! The exits started becoming over crowded, people rioted towards the stage.
We made our way to the exit; people had been
pushed down and were being trampled. Police resorted to using tear gas to break up the rioting
crowd. You dared not try to save someone, for if
you stopped you would be run down by the human
stampede as well.

    By the time we got out of the stadium, the
sun was shining brightly. The streets were steam-
ing. Several people were injured. The band, one
of the most popular rock bands in history, was
banned from ever playing in Florida again. There

we were, the four of us: me, my oldest niece, her girlfriend and for the sake of not using names, we'll call my buddy, the oldest brother, "bro." My niece's girlfriend was hot. She made me hot. I remember that.

Being raised by mostly women my whole life, I was intimidated by their sexuality. They had a cunning ability to use persuasive ways to get something done on their behalf. Needless to say, I was a bit of a late bloomer sexually. They had me figured out. It could be as simple as coercing me into doing some of their household chores to keeping my mouth shut about their personal actions. I would give first and seldom receive. Women: beautiful, sensuous, seductive, sexy, smart. I loved it. The thing was, a woman could make a fellow ache down in his soul to the point of failure or worse. Conversely, they could take a broken soul and mend it back to a full spirit. Revitalizing a person's life to the fullest. Women seem to have a strong sense of morality. When their mind is made up, there seems to be very little that may change it. A woman could be as brittle as fine china or as soft as a plush down pillow - it depended on your view at the time. Remember the old saying, "behind every great man stands a better woman." I've also heard such sayings as, "If they didn't have reproductive organs there would be a bounty on 'em." The saying you heard depended on if you heard it from someone who just fell in love and are looking towards marriage or one going through a divorce. Women throughout my life have been a blessing and a curse.

Back on the road to the trailer park we partied, making it home in what we considered safe shape meaning we made it without tickets or trouble.

I'm not sure what caused it, but my brother-in-law and sister got together again. We moved from the trailer park into a duplex not far away. The guys and I still ran together. We hung out more at the boys' house trailer than my home. Another Christmas came and by this time, my sister and brother-in-law were arguing again. It wasn't long and he moved out. This time, the girls went with him. I was left alone with my sister, who had no trust in me, so I was moved outside into the laundry room - a little rectangle room made of cinderblocks. She put a cot up. With some cinder block and wood, I built a couple of clothing shelves by the washer. I ate a lot of TV dinners, at least when I could get in to make one. I started skipping more school and selling more weed. Instead of hanging out in the trailer park, we hung out in a pool hall that at the time was transferring into a pinball room as well. We also picked up some more friends and our threesome turned into more of the avenue street gang.

It was in that pool hall that I met my first time love. She was small and petite, with brown hair and brown eyes. Wearing a tight set of jeans and flowery blouse, I still remember the first time I laid eyes on her. She was all I could see. Everything from the flashing lights of the pinball backboard to the wall itself vanished. I, the intimidated, couldn't even approach her. Oh, how I waited for her to come through those large clear glass doors. Of course, my insides vibrated and I couldn't figure out how to approach her; my stammering thoughts were sucked into a whirlpool down to the pit of my stomach instead of putting me into action. Somehow we got together and started being together. More than likely it was on her inducement.

Falling in young love, she brought me home to her house to meet her mother, brother and sister. Her mother was as beautiful as she was. Yes, she was considered beautiful to a young man's eyes with her full figure and strong, vibrant manner. They say to look at a woman's mother to see what you'll end up with. I hoped she turned out as beautiful. Her little sister had blond hair and blue eyes - one might think from a different dad. A little later down the road I met their father: blond hair, blue eyes. Genetics sure are amazing. Her little brother took after his mother in hair and eye color. They were good kids. Years later I heard her sister was married with kids and still lived in the same neighborhood.

Anyhow, her mother was really cool with us. With me being 17 and her the young age of 14, I started hanging out a little less with the guys and a little more with her and the family. Her mother, aware of my situation at home, decided I could go ahead and move in with them. I had to make a huge decision and face my sister. For all these

years of raising me, she had collected support
money from my father's Social Security. Once
again I was feeling demoralized, sleeping on a cot
in some washhouse, wearing worn-out jeans and
the same pair of too long shoes. The day came,
that day, the once a month day, the arrival of the
Social Security check. I hid in the bushes and
waited for the postman. Right on time, he opened
the mailbox, dropped the check in, and moved
down the street to his next stop. I knew I had to
be patient, but I couldn't afford to wait too long. I
gave the postman the distance of three mailboxes.
Knowing my sister would be counting on and have
plans for that money, she would be there promptly
after the postman passed as he pretty much arrived at the same time daily. I slipped out of the
brush near the duplex, acted like I was checking
the mail as regular as any other Joe. There was
the little manila envelope, with my name on it and
hers. I slipped back into the brush and waited. It
wasn't two minutes later and there came the red
Corvette. I could see her fan through the mail; too
far away to read her facial expressions. The red
Corvette turned around and sped off.

I had the check; I also had the shakes knowing I would eventually have to deal with my sister.
I had felt her hand or strap, not recently, but the
memory still lurked in my thoughts. She also could
and would give a good ass chewing. I headed out
of the brush when I felt it was all clear and went
back to my girlfriend's house. After contemplating
a bit on what to do, I called the guys and told them
what was going on. Of course, they helped me figure out my options. It was quite a bit of

unexpected money. It meant unexpected fun and pleasure.

We decided I should go into one of the major grocery stores and try cashing it. I signed her name, then my name on the check. I entered the store and asked whom I should see. They looked the check over, a government check with my name and identification. People may have been doing credit card theft or check cashing fraud at the time, but it was nothing like today's computer identity theft. They barely batted an eye as they handed over the cash. We were in 'em. With way more money than we were used to at once, we went and got plenty wasted. It was a good thing too, as I still had to face my sister's wrath.

The next afternoon I went to the duplex to confront my sister. When I told her what I had done she threw a fit. We argued intensely. For once I had her, whether she liked it or not. I simply stated that if she ever took the money from the mailbox again, I would make a call to a judge. She would have to produce years of receipts showing how the money was spent on my behalf. At least I had done a little bit of homework before executing this plan. I had her cold. From then on, which wasn't that much longer, she never touched the money. I definitely would now be living full time with my girlfriend or anywhere else besides the washhouse. I think my girlfriend's mom liked having a young man around. I was certainly good for doing odd jobs or what might be called the "honey do's," plus once a month I could contribute a little cash or fun for us.

By now I had quit school and decided money was more important. I was working on construction and still running with the avenue street gang. We weren't a gang of today's caliber. We didn't have guns and colored tattoos. We did have other little rival pin ball-pool hall gangs that we fought against, mostly with fists, sticks or the occasional chain would pop out. No one ever seemed to get too badly hurt. If they cruised our turf we would all run out of the hall and jump in the cars and start to chase the other pool hall gang down the city streets.

I remember one time when we caught up to them in stopped traffic. Ever heard of street fighting? Right in a major four-way highway, we went at it. That sort of thing though was fairly rare. Most of the time we were just chasing each other through the streets, hollering what we would do if caught up to them and visa versa.

In life there is nothing but the unknown. Life reveals itself moment by moment. You may think you can see your future, but you never truly know what's coming around the corner. Of course, having your goals established is wonderful. Taking great care in one's choices instead of quick decisions may, in the long run, pay off, depending on what lay through the choices. Your choice, before you realize the reality of the choice, can change your life forever. If only I had put my turn signal on, if I would have just got up in time. What those choices were, could be, might be, or hopefully never will be, has the possibility of reality. It could be a chance meeting while out one day to the store, park or shopping mall. Things that change one little course of our planned life may bring wonder or tragedy - even perhaps a tragic paralyzing situation due to a certain choice. You think, "If only I did it differently." Life and its uncertainties, more fragile than one thinks until you slip and cut your finger or have a near death experience. We should never take life for granted. Our situation in life can change with a simple phone call or a letter in the mail. It could be as difficult as just trying to be able to make it to the telephone or the mail box.

3

POUNDING the DOCKS

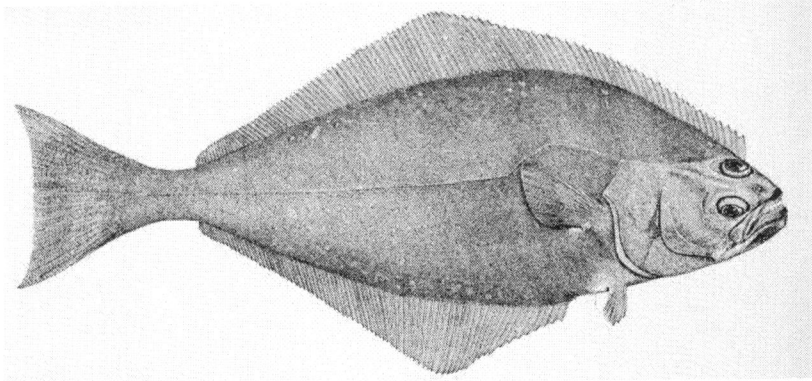

"Pound the docks and just keep pounding the docks," is the response that came from most of the fisherman I met. "If they tell you "no," just keep going back. Eventually something will happen, maybe someone will get hurt or sick. Green or not, a hand's a hand." For the first couple of days I pounded the docks. There were promises of possibilities and possibilities of promises.

With the dropping of the sunset came the chill. No more promises, no more possibilities; I was in need of refuge. I found it in the lobby of the Shee Atika where there was a sunken guest area. It was warm and comfortable with a couch and wide cushy chairs. Certainly they saw me;

could easily see that I was cold and getting desperately low for cash. Hell, I was so naive I didn't even bring a tent. I was also becoming good and familiar with the Columbia Bar, Ernie's and the P-Bar. I could go into the tavern for information, social necessity of the body, and for whatever other reason that may have turned up. But the value of alcohol goes up for the privilege. Drink two at the bar or six outside.

With my mornings being early so I wouldn't cause anyone any trouble, I'd head down to the Sitka Hotel café. The Sitka Hotel is the oldest hotel in Sitka (it might even be a historic building). A

woman named Lory owned the hotel and the café. Lory was a stout woman dressed in a white cook's uniform, white hair up in a bun; spackled stains of grease and unidentified batters on her uniform. She gave service with a smile and an interest in her patrons. I would get my usual, a cup of coffee and a pancake.

I had hoped that the day would be different. After I finished my breakfast, I headed down to the docks. There were three main harbors for me to travel back and forth on: Thompson Harbor, A.N.B., which means Alaska Native Brotherhood, and Crescent Harbor. Crescent Harbor was where I landed my first Alaskan fishing job.

Alaskan Crude

It was my day. An elderly couple, Barb and Sonny with a really nice 48-foot steel longliner or troller named the JETTA D, hired me on. There was a halibut-opening coming up and they would hire me for the season if the halibut trip worked out. I agreed and we shook hands. Sonny asked if that was all the gear I had. Looking at my old backpack, I said "Yes, sir." He immediately let me know that "sir" would not be needed in my vocabulary. Maybe it was from being in the Navy, but he made it clear. Then he said, "Get your gear. We'll show you your bunk and quarters."

They introduced me to the galley and the wheelhouse. Down below in the foc'sle were the bunks. Their bunk was wide enough for two. Mine was one of the two singles underneath. Right on! I had found a warm place and a job.

We were sitting at the galley table getting to know one another when Barb asked me what type of food I liked. I was into Mexican with hot sauces or basically anything easy and edible. Then she asked what type of alcohol I liked to drink. "Vodka," I say. About that time Sonny opened one of the lower cabinets and asked if I'd like to have a drink. "Sure," I replied. They didn't have the fifth size bottle rather they had the half-gallon. We had our drink and conversation. They told me to get acquainted with the boat and to fix out my bunk area, that they would be back in awhile. Excited, I got my bunk situated, gear stowed, came back up top, and started checking out the electronics.

In the early 1980's, we were just starting to phase out of using Loran A and going into using Loran C – which was the name of the signal vessels used to receive their position. (Loran is not like

what is currently used. Today, boats use a G.P.S.
Many are connected to a computer, some of which
are even further interfaced with an autopilot, radar, and depth sounder. Some systems are
programmed to follow the route you create and
make course corrections from one destination to
the other all on their own.)

Out on deck, the controls were at the side of
amidships; two levers, one for forward, neutral and
reverse, the other for speed and a couple valves
for what I didn't know. A large round metal wheel
with a groove in the center had two large black
hoses running into it. Come to find out, it was
called the shiv and was controlled by the valves at
amidships. It hauled the line with hydraulic power
back into the boat.

In the stern of the JETTA D was a two-foot
wide hole going the length of the beam, which was
from starboard to port or from side to side, with a
depth of four feet, and a platform for standing.
Each side had a metal bent two-inch rod with pul-
ley blocks hanging from them. When standing in
the area known as the "pit", the pulleys were
roughly hand high to the person in the pit. 5/16
stainless wire ran through the pulleys coming from
gurdies, which are also hydraulically driven. It was
sort of like an electric Penn reel going to a lead
ball. It was definitely intriguing. The lead balls
were stamped 50 and 60.

After a bit, Sonny and Barb returned with
three big brown bags full of food. There were Mexican fixings, sandwich material, snacks and one-
half gallon of vodka. Barb helped me get lined out
with the grub before she instructed me on the vodka - it was for me on the boat myself, not for

sharing with the rest of the crew in the fleet. I was a pig in shit, a clam at low tide, happy and spitting. They even bought me liquor!

I had a million questions. We had another drink and they assured me I would find out just how everything worked as long as I did "work out." The next day their son Matt came down to the boat early. I was up and at 'em; ready to fish. Matt introduced himself, let me know who was deck boss and who was grunt. He started explaining how things went with the longlining. First, there was a flagpole which floated in the water at about eight feet high with a little flag with the vessel's name on it and possibly a metal reflector on the very top so that in fog or snow it could be located with radar. Also tied to it were a couple of buoy balls, which were like tough exercise balloon balls going to the buoy line that went to the bottom for whichever depth you may be fishing. Tied between the buoy line and the main line or groundline, was an anchor to sink to the desired depth in the water. At the anchor started the groundline with hooks. We used snap-on hooks; so, after the panned out buoy line came the anchor – that was how you knew you were on the spot. After dumping the anchor over, the line started going out, and you would start snapping on a hook rig (A large circle hook on a three-foot leader with a snap that tightly fit the main line). The boat propelled forward at about three to five knots. You snapped a rig at about 18 to 21 feet apart. You did this for a couple miles until you came to the end of the set or reached the destination. Then you got another anchor, dumped it out, came up with the buoy line for whatever depth the skipper called out, and finished by tying on two buoys and a flagpole. Set made.

It sounded pretty much like a catfish trout line to me, just on a much grander scale. Matt drew it for me while we had coffee to get the morning started. The next few days we worked on getting the gear from his folks' place to the boat and thawing out the bait. We were baiting whole herring and chopped chum salmon. Big bait, big fish was the story I heard.

It was a 72-hour opening. Opening day, we lined up with the rest of the fishing vessels from the Canadian line out to the Aleutians. Time came, "Flag and bag" called the skipper. At this point I'm not sure who was skipper, Sonny or Barb. We let her go, made our first set, then we made our second set. I was pumped. The anchor was going over and the snapping of the hook rig happened every third swell. I was pumped with the anticipation of catching huge flat fish. We headed to an anchorage after making the two sets. "Gotta give 'em time to get on the line now," Matt said. We mopped up the deck on the way into anchorage. Anchored, we had a nice dinner with a few cocktails. Out on deck, Matt

suddenly looked at me, with his body flinching and said, "Feel that?"

Me, being surprised, replied "What?"

He said, "I just felt a big one get on." He got me. The greenhorn.

We all turned in with hope and expectations of a finding halibut on every hook.

The next morning I woke to the smell of coffee, bacon and breakfast. "Better eat while we can," Barb said with a smile. Sonny hauled the anchor. We started chugging our way to the first set of gear. We finished up with breakfast. Matt said, "Let's go and get the deck ready for hauling." We put coco mats on the top of the fish hold hatch. That was done so that while cleaning the fish they wouldn't slide around as much in the swell or rough sea. We slid the cleaning knives in their respective places and put the deck or fish checkers in. Checkers held the fish as they come aboard. We got our gear on, calf-high rubber boots, tough all weather rain gear, some type of gloves for hand protection whether vinyl or cotton over dishwasher gloves - different preferences for different people. A sharp get away knife shoved upside down into a small piece of garden hose taped to the forward breast strap of your bibs - for quick access to cut yourself free from injury or death. We also wore a belt knife.

As we pulled up on the flag and bags, Matt threw the grapple hook, which landed between the flagpole and buoys. We started pulling them over, grabbed the flagpole and hoisted it and the buoys aboard. We got the buoy line in the block, then into the shiv. We started hauling the buoy line in. Pretty quick the anchor came up. We freed the anchor from our ground line, the hooks started to come. Matt unsnapped the hooks, hung them on a rack.

As I stood by the starboard side rail, I peered down into the blue of the Pacific, waiting. Then I saw it. It looked like a big bed sheet coming up. Matt yelled, "Get a gaff, the first one's a big one. I may need your help." I was so excited I could have shit myself, but I tightened my bunghole and swallowed the knot in my throat.

"Once he breaks surface, I'll get my gaff in, then you. Only in the head," he said, "No body shot. We don't want to number two the fish."

The fish broke the surface; Matt slapped the point of the gaff in. The halibut was thrashing. I swung down hard to get my gaff in.

"Pull on the roll of the boat."

We do. The fish hit the deck, flopping and banging its large tail on the deck. Following the halibut came a beautiful, orange snapper known as yellow eye, as well as the occasional halibut. Fishing actually turned out to be few and far between. It was plenty to keep me busy at the time, bleeding and cleaning. Barb and Matt did most of the cleaning. I de-

nutted the fish and scraped the bloodline. Matt taught me how to ice the fish properly.

Alaskan Crude

After the set was hauled, we rebaited the hooks. We made another set for the following day to haul. Fishing was repetitious, as is so many jobs. It was the new challenge of every trip or every set that kept a fellow coming back. I was hooked. We fished our 72 hours, made five sets and had the time of my life. Good food, good drink, and good people. Plus, I was getting paid to fish.

We headed back to port. We had fished fairly close to Sitka so it didn't take but about five hours. Matt and I started scrubbing the boat on the way in. A bucket of soap, a deck brush, and hand brush applied with elbow grease. Sonny called into the fish plant. We got right in to unload. At the plant they hoisted our small fish out with cargo nets. The large fish, they used tail slings. After unloading, we shoveled out the leftover ice in the fish hold, scrubbed the boards and the fish hole out. While we did this, Sonny and Barb were at the scale shack getting weights on the fish. By the time we were done scrubbing, they were back to the boat with a check.

Tied up back at the dock in Crescent Harbor, I was about to learn about the "How big's yours?" syndrome. Every one compared their trip sizes. Not that I really gave a shit, I just went fishing and now had more money than I started with.

The next day, we started moving the gear back off the boat. The night before, the neighboring deckhand and I polished off that bottle of vodka and told our fishing stories. The gear got taken off and the boat got its final scrub down. Then we got paid. I grabbed my dirty clothes and headed straight to the bank smelling like a fish.

Alaskan Crude

Cashed my check - whatever it was, it was money. Smelling like a fish was common and a welcomed thing anywhere in town. The smell of fish meant money. You could just about bet your boots that the scruffiest, fishiest, smelliest guy in the bar would be getting laid that night 'cause he had had the big trip. Me, I was happy to have money again so I could order a drink and get some social necessity. Social was right.

After the opening, between one opener and another, I wasn't too busy. It was a couple weeks before the summer King salmon season opened. Others were getting ready to continue longlining out west in Kodiak, Sand Point, and on out to Dutch Harbor. The ideal seemed to be "work hard during the day, party hard all night." You had to be tough enough to get up in a grog, come to, and get back to it. Then you do it all over again 'til you heard the skipper say, "Cut her loose."

As the King salmon season came closer, I got broker. The Pioneer Bar, usually being the fisherman's choice of bars, was where I was one night when I was coerced into ringing the big brass bell without knowledge of the consequences. The bell went off, everybody started to cheer. The girls that were bar tending went to serving drinks to everyone in the bar. Finally, they brought me mine. Mary, the head bartender at the time, served me. She came up, with those extra large set of boobs on her small framed body and said, as she sat my drink down, "That'll be $90.00."

"What?"

"You rang the bell, you got to pay."

"Mary, I don't have $90.00".

"You pay or go to jail - that's the deal." She was staring hard at me. I was wearing a gold chain. Then she said, "That will do," pointing to the chain. I took it right off - I definitely didn't want to go to jail.

"You can have it back when you come pay the bill," she says with a sharp hard glance straight into my eyes.

Days went by and so did the next couple weeks. Sonny and Barb still kept me fed and liquored. Each day there would be some type of deck or gear work to prepare for King salmon season. We were to head to the Fairweather grounds, north of Sitka. The grounds contain large, upwelling pinnacles with edges and flats. It was an 18-hour run to the fishing grounds. Along the coastline was the Fair-weather Mountain Range, a wondrous scenic coast of glaciers, rivers, and snow covered mountains that stretched into the mist and above the clouds back into the sunshine – reaching over 5,000 feet to the top.

There was only one anchorage between Icy Point and Yakutat - Lituya bay. In order to get inside the bay you have to cross a sand bar. No matter if you are crossing it at high slack water or on a nice day, you are going to ride a couple, three small curlers. While doing so, you have to stay on course within the range markers that lead you into the bay. Once inside the bay, Cenotaph Island sits directly in the center. To the port side, the mountain is stripped two-thirds of the way up, which is the mark of a deadly tsunami from 1958. Floating in the water are chunks of blue crystals.

Sonny told me to get the dip net. We scooped up some million-year-old cocktail ice. As we neared the back of the bay, there were three major glaciers coming down to the shoreline: two large ones on each side of the bay, a smaller one in the center. The receding glacier's face broke off in great, massive chunks. It sounded like thunder. The boat rocked in its wake. We drifted around, dipped up some million-year-old ice for the million-year-old cocktail. We admired the glaciers and pondered the enormous force of a tsunami wave, sent our condolences to the ones who died and the ones who'd lived through it.

Knowing that a big day loomed ahead, we headed out to the fishing grounds. Back in town, I'd heard all about the Fairweather grounds and how good you could do there. Forty to fifty nautical miles off shore lay the Fairweather grounds, from Ham Bone to West Bank. Our job was to find good sign of King salmon. Getting the gear ready,

Barb and I threaded salted herring on treble hooks. We had hoochies of various colors, shining fishing spoons of chrome and brass-copper, large wooden plugs that looked like bait running wild as if another fish was already after it.

That evening, before the King salmon opener, we lay drifting offshore with the magnificent view of the Fairweather range. So massive, it

looked as if you could easily swim to it. Following tonic time, we grubbed up then to bed. Morning came once again with excitement, expectation and hope.

Barb and I got back into the troll pit. She started showing me how to put the gear out, count the depth of wire and how to work the gurdie controls. As soon as the gear was deployed, the fish started to hit. Sonny came back and Barb went in the wheelhouse. Sonny was fixing to show me how to run the gear, play the fish, properly stun and gaff the fish aboard the boat. Morning had started out good. Sonny showed me then left me to it. It was exhilarating playing those beautiful Alaskan King salmon. Barb came back out on deck and taught me to gill, gut and clean. Fish handling on a commercial troller is of the utmost importance.

By mid day I got her dialed: running the gear, landing and bleeding the fish, then getting them cleaned and iced. Back in the troll pit, I let out the port heavy, thinking I was the man; the stainless main wire goes out with a 60-pound lead weight. I snapped the leaders on, threw the lure or spoon out - mistake. I was thinking I was faster than I was. I felt the sharp tip sinking deep into my thumb, striking the bone. I didn't reach the valve in time so the reel of stainless wire looked like a bird's nest with the gurdie still panning the wire out. Meanwhile, I was holding a 60-pound cannon ball by my thumb that was dragging in the water. Hollering "help" as loud as I could, but with being stretched over the rail, the ocean could hear me better than the captain. By then, the Number 8 hook had taken a full bite and came out towards the tip of my thumb, still hanging on to a nice chunk of meat. Finally, they heard me, came out, and cut me free of the leader. Sonny had Barb take me to the wheelhouse to check the damage. There it was - a big chrome spoon hanging off the end of my thumb. We cut the glove off my hand exposing the truth. Sonny got the bolt cutters to free the spoon from the hook. That left the hook. I was all for turning my head while one of them sliced open the meat of the thumb. No takers, and I couldn't bring myself to do the slicing. So the de-cision was made to go back to town to have it removed.

Alaskan Crude

Besides fucking up the trip, by the time I got back to town, everyone already knew about the boat that was coming back from the grounds with an injury. It took the doctor one swift lick with a scalpel and me several swift kicks from fellow fisherman to live down the mistake I made by not releasing the hook before I snapped it onto the troll wire - all of which caused the boat to have to return to port during an opening.

We spent the rest of the King salmon season off the Coast of Kruzof Island outside of Sitka. Fishing was fairly bleak. I loved conking every one that took the hook. After King season was over and the boat scrubbed and clean, I was paid.

I headed directly to the Pioneer Bar to pay my tab for ringing the bell. Got my got chain back and at which time I proceeded to get fucked up, the bar full of patrons. People six packing other people (six drinks at once in front of a person). Guys pulled out wads of hundreds, forgetting their change as they traveled from one end of the bar to the other, ordering more drinks. One thing I noticed was I was short on that fat wad of hundreds. So I got to bullshitting with someone - I could see being broke again soon. I started to mention the massive cash flow being passed around. This guy said, "Well, if you want some of that I know a highline freezer troller that's looking for a hand. He stays out until he fills the boat or the season ends."

The following day, even though feeling bad not just from the hard and harsh drinking of the night before, but also the bad feeling came from me searching out another job. I found Ron standing at the top of ANB Harbor, about 5'8" or 5'9", wavy brown shoulder length hair, beard and mustache, with tenseness about him that you could see through his body language. As I approached him, he looked at me with rather mean eyes.

"I hear you might be looking for a hand," I say.

"What's your name?"

"Charlie."

"Can you clean fish, do any navigating, read radar, find yourself on a chart?"

"Sure can," I said thinking to myself-thanks to Sonny and Barb and their efforts of preparing me for a full troll season with them.

"Where's your gear?" he asks.

"On the JETTA D in Crescent Harbor."

He was holding a piece of electronics in his hand. "I'll drop this off then we'll get your gear." It shocked the shit out of me. You mean *now* I'm thinking. I just agreed.

Coming up on the JETTA D I was feeling like a traitor. Ron didn't seem to give a shit about taking someone else's deckhand. I went in and sadly broke the news to them. It was sudden and without warning. It was distasteful all the way around. What else could I say? What could they do? I gathered my gear. I introduced them to Ron who looked impatient. Sonny and Barb looked disappointed and unhappy with me. Over the rail, up the dock, I went with Ron. Later I came to find out there was usually quite the turnover with deckhands swapping from boat to boat after the King salmon opener.

I was a smoker, so I lit up a cigarette. Ron looked at me.

"There's no smoking on the boat," he said.

He waited to spring this on me after I had already quit my other job.

"The tar and nicotine comes out of the pores on your hands, you'll be handling the gear. It affects the fishing. You can get some Redman and chew if you like."

Now I'm thinking tobacco DTs. But I agreed and kept in mind that he was a highline troller, one of the best. We walked down to the ANB harbor, everyone was busy with projects: regearing for Cohos or silver salmon, King salmon had brought the first money into the troll fleet.

The MYSTIC was a 60-foot ketch sailing vessel converted into a freezer troller moored on the south outside end of the harbor. As we proceeded down to the far finger of the dock, the voices of men started to become amplified with every other word being "fuck" or a belittling statement. The captains pushed the crew, the crew scowled back; each worked the other for their weakness or to know the others' strength. The harbor was a much coarser harbor than the one I had just left.

The MYSTIC was black and beautiful. The double masted rig had a long stainless bowsprit. Up the forwar mast was a crow's nest for look out. The wheelhouse was low and sleek. We entered the wheelhouse cabin, then went down into the lower levels that held a large galley: diesel oil stove, double sinks, a galley table that would comfortably seat four to six. Towards the aft were three staterooms, two on the port side and one on the starboard side. Ron opened the door to the starboard cabin. "This one's yours." he said.

As we had boarded the boat, his tension grew. He grew eager to depart for the fishing grounds, seeing as to how he had filled the position. Up on top, he went forward, lifted up a hatch and hollered down. Up came Terry out of the freezer hold, a scruffy, heavyset fellow with Levi overalls, hairy and bearded. Hairy and bearded virtually describes half of the fleet. Not me, at least not yet. Ron introduced us; let Terry know I'll now be the new first mate. Ron's pay scale went according to rank of position. I got eight percent and Terry, six. Ron made clear the stipulations on my eight, he would pay me five until the end of the season, and then, if I stuck it out, I would collect on the other three percent. The same went for Terry except it would cost him half his wages. Ron called it a retraining fee.

Ron was like a busy bee collecting pollen. The Sitka electronics shop had told Ron his electronics would be fixed and ready the next afternoon. Salmon trips that are processed and frozen at sea can take weeks. The good thing is you're not in town often enough to spend your money as fast or faster than you make it. Stay and make it pay, when this vessel left, that's what it did. The other part of the saying is "run and have fun." Chase the fish up and down the coast stopping in every port, spending, drinking and having fun. You could possibly find yourself without a way out come late fall.

Ron proceeded to give me my duties: cooking and food shopping were on my immediate list for tomorrow. I was informed that I'd have

$400.00 to shop with for possibly a month of fishing, with only a $20.00 allowance for meat. In the morning, I went shopping, sticking to the criteria buying only hamburger to get the most bang out of my buck. Back at the boat, I stowed the grub away, filled the fresh water tank, and prepared for sea. "No drinking, no smoking, no drugs." Fuck it. I snuck a quarter ounce of the mean green - just too much "no" for one motherfucker to put up with. The days started early and the evenings lasted almost until tomorrow. Ron pretty much lived on the Fairweather grounds.

Off once more to the Fairweather grounds, the 60-foot ketch bucked into the westerly swell against a westerly wind. Ron kept us on a schedule of two men up at a time, one down. Outside of Cross Sound on the Spencer Spit, Ron tossed the gear in and told me to wake up Terry. I went down, rapped on the cabin door, and hollered for him to get up. He acknowledged me. I went back on deck.

Ron said, "Is he up"?

"Yes, I woke him."

I could feel a heavy tension in the air between the two as it was even in town. About 10 minutes went by. Ron said, "Go see what he's doing."

I went below - the dude never got up. Once again, I banged on the cabin door, this time I opened the door to be sure he was sitting up. Terry's basic job was to do the first cleaning of the salmon. I would follow up with the heading and final cleaning before freezing and glazing.

Finally, he was up on deck. Ron cut lose on Terry, telling him how fucking worthless he was and to get to work. I was like, "Whoa!" I had heard those guys on the dock hollering and belittling each other, but they seemed to enjoy it. This was just rude. Ron was the only one to run the gear or catch the fish. I realized we were processors, not fisherman.

As the first week went on, it became more and more repetitious. I would run the MYSTIC through the night and build gear, sharpen gaffs, get us to our destination. Also it was my time to slip in a snack - a toke. I bunked down in the morning as the gear went out. I got a couple, three hours before getting back up. Long, long days. I made breakfast while it was Terry's time down. Ron, after a couple, three hours, told me to go get Terry up.

Terry didn't respond fast enough for Ron, once again as usual. Ron just started screaming vile shit on Terry. Terry, adjusted to the verbal abuse, just stared not even seeing or hearing or caring. This time Ron got out of the pit went below decks to Terry's cabin. Comes up with Terry, screaming, "From now on, motherfucker, you'll sleep on the galley floor. I'll kick you awake if you don't move your ass." So it became, the fucker had to sleep on that hard ass floor. Ron didn't direct all of his anger at Terry. He would holler at me a little too, but he really needed me more for the navigation and the final product of salmon.

Alaskan Crude

As the days rolled on, the fishing went from being as dry as a popcorn fart to fucking more fin-fish than I'd ever seen. Ron turned more vicious and became what the fellow at the bar said - a salmon killer. I see him now as a morale killer as well. Anything Terry was told to do wasn't good enough. We had a hydraulic hose go bad and leak. Once Ron and I got it repaired, it was left up to Terry to clean up the mess. A rag fell in the shaft alley. Terry, of course, didn't notice. Ron came down for an inspection and there was a rag going round and round on the shaft. He blew his top. He came charging up topside, looked at Terry and said, "Come the fuck over here." Terry frantically, slowly, shivering, went towards Ron. Ron jumped his shit about the rag on the shaft. As he's hollering, he shouts, "Grab your fucking ankles." I'm watching all this thinking, "Don't do it." But, what the heck as long as he's not fucking with me like that - a fellow has to make his own choice. Terry did, he bent over and grabbed his ankles. Ron planted that knee-high rubber boot to center of Terry's ass and knocked Terry forward three feet.

From that day on through the rest of the trip, the abuse got worse for Terry. He was never good enough. His asshole must have gotten tattered up due to the daily kicking.

Alaskan Crude

The trip had been long and relentless. It showed me a whole other side of fishing I never expected to see. After a hard spent 21 days, we were full. We headed back down the coast to Sitka.

Ron had a heart for Rosie who owned Rose's Bar and Grill in Pelican, Alaska. Rosie is a wonderful woman who could always drink most men under the table. We had stopped in and drop off fish to Rosie, have a beer and a burger, then be on our way to Sitka. It was only eight more hours until the relief of town. Our turn around was to be quick. Terry would not longer be trapped to the tyrant. I would quit as soon as we unloaded, scrubbed and got paid. If only I were fully paid. There was enough time to get good drink or two in and score another bag of weed. Even Ron knew we deserved 24 hours.

Alaskan Crude

After two days of boat work, we headed back to the Fairweather grounds for our last trip, the fall trip. The silver salmon were getting to their largest. We were switching to fishing more inshore, in front of the wild salmon rivers, the Dangerous, Seatuk and Saook. Once again, out at sea and fishing, Ron turned tyrant, working us into mental and physical exhaustion. Yet each day I had to acknowledge him as a relentless troller. Terry, taking an unimaginable amount of verbal, physical and mental abuse found that it was no longer satisfying to Ron to have him bend over and grab his ankles. He now got a daily head dipping in what we called the leach tank - a drum of congealing water that is used in the processing of salmon. Terry, drug by his beard to the tank, while under the attack of severe verbal abuse, would be forcefully shoved into the leach tank and be held in by pulling on his beard and the hair on his head.

Alaskan Crude

About the time he would be ready to suck water, Ron would pull him up, screaming and ask him if he was going to fuck up again. By the time Terry could get his breath, Ron would shove him back down into the tank. This went on for weeks.

Ron never physically touched me, though he would bitch me out if I weren't at the perfect spot I was supposed to be when he got up in the morning. I had hardened by his ruthlessness. I loved the sea as well as the fishing. I thought, "Fine, if this is how fishing really is, I'm good with it. I may not live long, but I'll live with and against the elements, even if the elements include fucking tyrants like Ron."

One time though, he did cause me to see red. It was morning and my turn to go down, to get three hours of shuteye. I awoke groggy, unsure of even where I was, but I could hear screaming. I was sitting up and out of nowhere I got hit in the head followed by a sharp pain in my foot. With a hand on my head, I looked down at my bleeding foot. I went fucking nuts. There, lying by my foot was a 3/4-inch nut and bolt with a tuna jig used for retrieving broken fishing lines. I grabbed it up and stormed up on deck. When we laid eyes on each other, Ron knew I wasn't grabbing my ankles. I hauled back with that jig, Ron crouching down, as I released it with all my might. I missed. I looked at him and said, "Some body don't come back." After that, he knew one of us would die if that shit continued. He became fairly mild mannered with me, just doubled up on the daily abuse of Terry. It even got to a point where I wanted to physically abuse Terry.

Alaskan Crude

Getting fuller day by day and counting the days left 'til September 21st, the date salmon season officially ended, we were fishing the Seatuk River above Yakutat. Fishing was phenomenal. Huge silver salmon were coming in - two to three hundred fish a day for a week. "Praise be!" were my thoughts that last week. We were halfway through the last week when we were headed into the sun, just pulling, cleaning, and processing salmon. I was in the galley changing from freezer gear back into fishing gear when all of a sudden I was thrown against the galley lockers. I looked through the portholes and saw another vessel grind against the starboard side of the boat. I hit the deck in case of objects coming through the portholes. The grinding stopped. I ran up on deck.

We had collided with a wooden troller, taking his starboard trolling pole out as well as a large chunk of his flying bridge. The MYSTIC'S starboard pole bent crooked and tangled with the other vessel. Both vessels' bolt cutters come out, freeing the rigging from one another. There was hollering and cussing across from vessel to vessel. The other vessel gathered their rigging and got their trolling pole. They headed in for repairs, their season now over. Ron was relentless – we Jerry-rigged the starboard side so we could continue.

We finished the season with a bang. Once again, Ron managed to fill the boat. Back in Sitka we unloaded, scrubbed up, and actually got paid in full. I let Terry know if he wanted to press charges against Ron, he could own the boat. All he wanted was his money and to get back to wherever he came from.

Alaskan Crude

Ron moved on to fish the Hawaiian Islands. Before he left he said he could use a foot loose and fancy-free guy like myself. I told him I would think about it. He said he would be staying in the Sheffield Hotel. "Was he out of his fucking mind?" I couldn't stand the guy. That night I went out drinking, found a girl to party with, a smoker, a heavy drinker, and of course, a lover. I brought her to the boat, took her to my stateroom, got drunk, smoked cigarettes and fucked. Early the next morning we left, me with all my gear in hand, and left that fucking tyrant to clean the mess. The vessel eventually caught fire and sunk somewhere off the Hawaiian Islands. Ron and the crew survived.

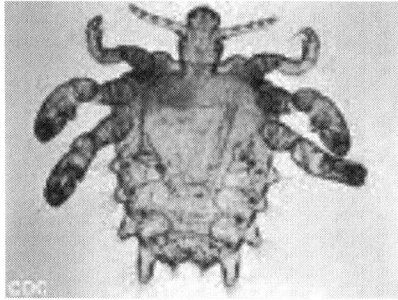

THE DEADLIEST SNATCH

At the end of the season, a girl who had followed me from Seattle to Sitka came down to the harbor and found me. She showed up right before we were going to untie and be on our way to Yakutat for a late season black cod opening. "You wanna get laid before you head out?" she asked. Of course, as any mariner knows, it's a sign of good luck, or at least it's said to be, to get some tail before going fishing. I had a little 33-foot double ender tied up in the same harbor, so I hopped off the stern of my captain's boat and we trotted on down to my rig in a bit of a rush. I didn't want my captain to yell at me for being late. Usually we would get an ass chewing if we were late due to alcohol; however, being late because of sex, most of the time, was forgivable, but not always.

The girl and I did our thing and said our goodbyes. Then I went back to the boat. All's well that ends well, I was thinking.

Off we headed to the fishing grounds. It took a couple of days to get that far up North and on our way we did the standard things: baited up and bullshitted with each other. The sea was fair and everything was working fine with the vessel. However, during one of my wheel watches, it really started to come to my attention that a small but very powerful army was infiltrating me.

I needed to confirm my suspicions. I found a flashlight, pulled down my pants, and started look- ing through my pubic hair. I saw one of the soldiers, caught and killed it with my fingertips. I pulled my pants up so there was no way for the lit- tle fuckers to escape, but I didn't know what to do. I knew that I would have to come clean with my captain and the rest of the crew, but how? Every- one knows that when sleeping in close quarters things travel, especially living things.

The next day I was really sweating it. I didn't know how to drop the bomb! We anchored up behind Kayak Island one night and right after dinner I decided to tell the captain.

"Skip? Can I speak to you in private?" We went out on deck. "I think I have crabs. Well, no, I <u>know</u> I have crabs."

He looked at me and said, "No, you don't."

"Yes, I do!" I replied.

He went to the back of the wheelhouse and returned with a large, very large, spoon and a tin of Bag Balm. He opened the container, scooped some out, and told me to put it on. Bag Balm is used to soften sore teats on dairy cows; it takes down the swelling from the milking machines, and fishermen use it for swollen hands and to try and prevent fish poisoning. "We'll smother the little devils", the captain said.

After the crew was informed of the situation, they let me know if they carried the plague, too, that I would suffer for it. They would have no choice but to pummel me because they would go home and explain it to their wives.

Throughout the whole fishing trip, I was in total anguish; I had a war going on in my pants and I was on the verge of war with the rest of the members of the vessel. I used the word "members" because they were becoming real dicks towards me. It seemed like we were no longer part of the same crew.

We set our gear the next morning and gave it some time to soak. It was a 48-hour opening. So, with our soak time, we were 6 to 8 hours into it; flag and bag time. It was time to haul the fish in. I'm sure we set enough gear to keep us busy the remaining hours, during which time the crew were thinking shit on me and I was thinking shit on her. In a situation of this magnitude, I just couldn't wait for this to be over. I always stayed up on top, away from the foc'sle to keep the possibility of contamination to a minimum down in the sleeping quarters.

We worked through the night and then through the day and again into the night. Finally, the next dawn we saw what would mark the end of our search for prosperity, at least for this endeavor. It was the year of the Exxon Valdez oil spill so we headed to Cordova to sell our mighty catch and possibly get work on the clean up that Exxon was throwing money at.

First thing I did when we reached land was to head for the pharmacy. I got some Rid-X and a shaver. I also got a room above the local tavern, anticipating a need for several drinks after doctoring myself up. The bar was large and definitely old. My room was small, but equipped with a shower, TV, and a crapper. So I got busy. This time I would be the victor of the war.

After I got cleaned up, I went downstairs and proceeded to have a few, and then a few more. With me being me, I got to talking to this fellow and one things led to another. He asked me if I want to split a gram. Well, I was drunk and a pick-me-up sounded pretty good. So, off he left and returned again a bit later.

Soon after the fellow returned, three good-looking women came in and called him over. I could easily see them talking in the wall-to-wall mirror behind the bar. The guy headed back over to me and said, "Those girls say you are a narc."

"What?" I scoffed.

"They say they've seen you before. Buddy, I don't know what your deal is, but as far as we're concerned, your next destination is a crab pot."

I didn't want any trouble, but I couldn't help but to shout out "Bull shit!" All of a sudden, I couldn't get another drink, so I headed to the next bar across the street. No sooner do I get in there, I turn around and there they are: the women and the guy. They said something to the bartender and I couldn't get a drink in there either.

I was feeling increasingly nervous, so I split from the three and headed for the boat rather than my room. Even if one of the crew is upset with you, a bond is forged so they were definitely my best option. Since I left my belongings back in the room, all I had left on the boat was my .44 magnum and a sleeping bag. I got up on the wheelhouse roof and waited there. No one showed up.

Exxon ended up not hiring wooden vessels due to oil absorption. I was glad to hear that because it meant we could get the fuck out of Cordova and go back home to Southeast Alaska.

Later, I found out that Bag Balm may soften your junk and Rid-X get rid of crabs, but you should always have a piece of devil's club root to ward off a woman's bad juju.

5

STRANGE SENSE OF HUMOR

Alaska's fishing fleet had its fair share of cha-
racters. One such character was Hard Lay Ray.
Loved to drink, smoke, laugh, and sing. He didn't
like to be pressed or messed with. Heart of gold
but would beat you with a gaff hook or whatever
might be handy if you stole from him or insulted
him. His sense of humor was naturally crude.
Hired on as a cook on a Southeast Salmon seiner,
he was the first up in the morning, making coffee,
getting the bacon going. When he was all done

and left to his own thoughts he started to think of how he could fuck with the crew.

Sipping through his coffee, he started thumbing through a new issue of Playboy. Opened up the centerfold, he held her up. As he admired, a thought came to him. He took the photograph, tacked her up on the galley wall. I'm sure while flipping the bacon he envisioned the humor of his own joke. Right before he hollered down in the foc'sle that breakfast was ready, he reached down into his ass crack, got the stink of shit on his finger. He wiped it right on the centerfold's pussy.

As the guys came out of the foc'sle and gathered around the galley table, Ray poured the coffee. The guys immediately noticed the centerfold. They started bullshitting about getting laid and worried that their girl was while they were gone fishing. In Alaska, there's a saying: "You don't lose your old lady; you just miss your turn." They were going on about the centerfold.

Ray said, "Check it out; it's one of those new scratch and sniff centerfolds that Playboy puts out." One of the crew reached up, scratched her pussy, and stuck his nose up there.

"Damn, that smells like shit."

Ray told him, "You must have scratched the wrong hole." He looked at him and laughed. The background echoed with laughter.

We were sitting at the bar drinking and laughing, me listening to Ray's bullshit. A fellow sat down beside Ray and said, "Sorry to hear you're dying of cancer." Ray looked at him as he took a big long drag off an unfiltered cigarette. "Hell, dying of cancer! I'm living with cancer." Ray tilted his beer, took a swill. He turned, looked at me, ignoring the other fellow now and said grinning, "You ever been with a woman so nasty she woke you by smell? Well, I have," he said. "I just eased out and away from her not to wake her. I quickly get my shit and when I took a good look at her, not only was she ugly, the only clean spot on her was about the size of a 50 cent piece right on her tit where I had sucked the dirt off of her last night. I went to brush my teeth, picked up the tube of toothpaste, started brushing my teeth and fuck, it tasted so terrible I spit the stuff in the sink. I picked up the tube. It was the bitch's vaginal cream." I laughed with him and thought, I wonder what she would have told her girlfriends if she had woken up first?

Ray died living with cancer in Petersburg, Alaska.

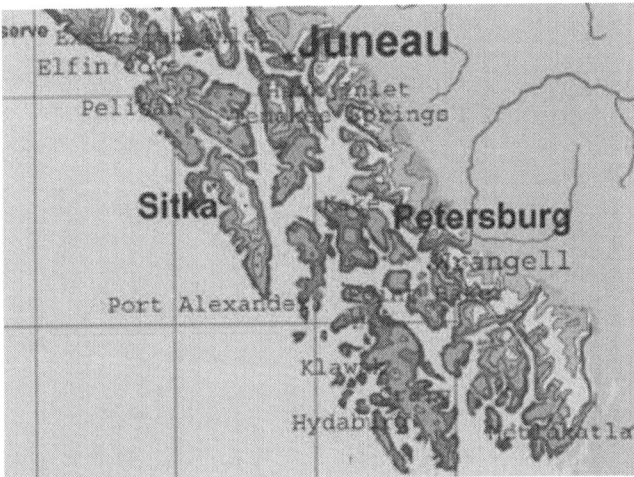

Alaskan Crude

6

WINTER TIME FISHING

Winter gillnetting for mackerel and longlining for swordfish off the central coast of Florida were my wintertime fisheries. I'd fly back to Florida like big daddy War bucks and it wasn't long before I'd have my shirt off, pulling on a gillnet. It doesn't take long to grub up and get back out on deck and it doesn't take a seasoned party animal long to go through his wad, and know it's time to get back out and make another withdrawal from the bank of the ocean.

We were fishing off Cape Canaveral, gillnetting king mackerel; fishing was slow to nil. The NASA space shuttle <u>Challenger</u> stood upright and ready for launch. Night after night, we cruised the sandy shores looking for a school of mackerel. The skipper, younger than me, and the crew, two young fellows straight out of the Appalachian hill country were found living out of their car and looking for warmer weather. The crew had a blond hair, blue eyed, well-tanned surfer kid as well.

The water was so full of phosphorous at night that if you came across a school of fish, it would light the water to a brilliant light blue. With the excitement of letting the net go. Then the disappointment to pull in trash fish and just plain old pieces of trash. We were really getting tired of finning dog shark and picking out the blue fish. Most of the time, when we would catch a king mackerel the sharks had gotten to it first.

One night while hauling the net back in, the greenhorn skipper kept backing down on the net, given this is what you're supposed to do. However, you're not supposed to back over the net so that it gets in your propeller. With the net now stuck in the propeller, the engine stalled out. Our fearless captain came out looking dumb founded even though we were hollering that the net was traveling under the stern. Floating adrift, everyone looked at each other. I brought up the possibility of diving down to the propeller and cutting the monofilament web loose and away. The skipper thought it was a good idea except that he didn't want to do the diving. We all knew from the fish in the net that the sharks were feeding off the net.

I looked at the two hillbillies. I doubted that they had swum in anything deeper than a bathtub. The surfer kid looked fairly promising. For me, it wouldn't have been my first time down to cut away debris from the propeller, but I didn't want to be a patsy. I figured that at least the water was warm and clear. As long as the sharks maintained feeding off the fish in the net, I only had to worry about getting caught up in loose web or my greenhorn skipper turning on the engine and putting it in gear, sucking me into the whole mess. I sharpened a serrated knife, took off my boots, put on my tennis shoes. I told the skipper that he had better stay away from that starter key, even if I had to take it from the ignition.

I took a couple of deep breaths, got over the rail, looked back at the fucking guy, and jumped

off the port side - the net was laying to starboard. Definitely not enjoying the thought of the sharks, I tried to shuck off all of the thoughts going to my brain except my project. There was a small chop, enough to bounce the stern up and down. With a deep breath, I pushed myself under the stern. The web led me right to the propeller. In order to cut the web free, I had to get a good hold on something or somehow fasten myself to the rudder. The action of the boat going up and down could beat the barnacles into your skin, causing you to bleed which would of course, act as shark attractant. I quickly surveyed the situation and got away and came up for a breath. They were all staring over the side.

"Yup, you got it in the wheel." As I was treading in the water and listening to the "Yea who", I said, "I gotta do it before I lose my nerve."

Alaskan Crude

To the stern with a couple of deep breaths, I
pushed under and swam down to the rudder. I got
a good hold and started cutting toward that stainless tail shaft. The boat was surging mildly enough
to be a nuisance. Out of breath, I had to go back
up. Popping up, there were my four buddies staring at me. I gave my progress report and once
again went to the stern, pushed under, got myself
fastened to the rudder, and cut as hard and as fast
as I could. By putting my left arm between the
rudder and the rudderpost, I was able to help rip
the cut monofilament from the propeller and shaft,
freeing the net from the boat.

 With the hydraulics engaged, we started to
haul the net. I can't remember if I was on the cork
line or the lead line. It wasn't too long and I was
looking at the other guys and they were looking at
me. I hollered out to the skipper, "You're backing
over the net!" The fucking guy kept backing down
the net, making it impossible for us to keep up. It
seemed to be only minutes when the engine stalled
out. Once more, the net was wound around the
propeller. He came out like he didn't know how
that could have happened. Looking at me while
I'm looking at him, I said "Fuck that, you got it in
wheel, I think you should get it out." He protested
that he needed to be topside. One old timer once
told me that you should never do something for
someone else that they're not willing to do themselves. This seemed to be one of those cases.

 Completely pissed off now, I stand next to
the rail looking on shore at the Challenger, the
bright light pounding against it. It was a clear
night in Cape Canaveral, Florida. I was disgusted
at the thought of going through that dive again. I

figured my odds of an accident probability just got cut in half. I turned away and said to the skipper, the crew listening intently, "The only way I'll do it again is if each one of these guys tries first." Then I threw in that most times a person gets paid a little something extra to rise above.

The skipper started making promises. I looked at my deck mates, all saucer-eyed and said, "Somebody better get a knife." The more alpha male of the two Appalachian fellows said, "I'll go." "Good," I said, then got the life ring out and into the water. He was definitely scared; he had already seen the barnacle scratches on me and knew the sharks were on us. I tried to prepare him for what was going on when he got there. I told him that he was to fasten himself and cut like a mad man. The net was laid just like before, off the starboard side. He jumped in. Finding no bottom to stand on, he surfaced, those saucer eyes now the size of dinner plates. I assured him he was alright. "Just relax and catch your breath." He got a hold of the ring, calmed down a bit. It was time for him to try to clear the net. He cut loose from the ring and got over to the port stern of the boat. I encouraged him and said, "When the boat surges up, get under it, take a deep breath. When it comes down, put your hand up. It will help force you down, then swim to the rudder."

The stern went up, he went under the boat, and as the stern came down he disappeared under. There were maybe two or three surges when he popped out from under the hull. Big eyed and breathing hard, he was tired. Looking down at him, I said, "Well, did you get any?"

"Never made it."

"You're already in the water. Want to try again?"

"Okay" he said. Back to the stern, the surge took the boat. Under he went and out he popped with the next upward surge. He looked up and said, "I'm done." "Good job trying," I said, "let's get you out of there". We hauled him up. The other two did not want to try so I reiterated that each one had to try. The alpha male counterpart decided that he would go next. I say "Take the knife, try to get down there and cut that web." I threw the life ring. The kid was about ready to shit his shorts. I said, "You at least have to get in and try." He looked at his partner, then at me, and jumped off. He swam better than I thought. "Just get the ring, catch your break," I said. He kicked around a bit and calmed down. I asked, "Alright, ready to give it a try?" He shook his head yes. We pulled him towards the stern. I asked him, "You know what to do?" He cut loose from the life ring, got his hand on the hull. As the surge brought the boat up, he tried to go under. The boat came back down and cracked him on the head. It scared the hell out of him. He grabbed on to the orange life ring for his life. "Okay, good enough" I said.

The skipper came back and put in his two cents. It was like pennies in a wishing well, didn't mean shit to me, just someone else's dream or wish. The only two cents I cared about were mine. All of the crew had to try before I was going back in. With mate Number 2 back aboard, there was only one left to go - the blue eyed blond-haired fit looking surfer kid. I had a hidden hope inside of me that he could swim like a fish. When the kid hit the water, he looked like a fish all right - a baitfish injured and floundering around on the surface. Even the two hillbillies treaded water reasonably well. We needed to get this kid back into the boat before he brought more sharks. They respond all too well to splashing and thrashing around. So we drug his pretty boy ass back out of the water and into the boat.

The deed was once again passed to me and I did not like the thought of going through the whole ordeal again. It made me feel better knowing that the rest of them had at least felt the fear that we all now had in common. I took the knife, threw the ring with disgust and hopped over the side. It took me a few times down but I finally got the web free. I was a hero once more. I told the skipper that if it happened again there was no fucking way I was going down again.

We started hauling the net, got it in and stacked on the deck. The relief of seeing the tail end come over the roller pleased us all. It had been a long night. I found myself staring out at the space shuttle Challenger. The launch date was getting close. Tied back up along the sea wall, we shut down and got some shut eye. Tomorrow there would be a lot of mending to do.

I woke in a sweat – it was mid day and I smelled the coffee. Coming out of the forecastle, it felt good to have a breeze pass over my body. With a cup of coffee in hand, I walked out on deck with the sun pounding down intensely. The Appalachian guys were coffeeing up back on the stern. We looked at each other and held up our cups to one another. The skipper came out and said, "We'll have breakfast then we will back haul and mend the net." Good enough.

It wasn't long until the kid popped out of the hole. With breakfast over, it was time to get to it. We threw the lead line over the roller, grabbed a hold, pulled down, and got the net coming up and over the roller. Stacking lead line onto the port and cork line to the starboard, we checked the net for rips and tears. We mended the small tears and got to the hack holes from the knife of the night before.

As the heat of midday turned into the coolness of evening, we got word that the Challenger was on standby for take off. All traffic in and out of the Cape came to a stop. Before you could exit the Cape jetty, there, just like a big traffic light, stood the signal for all to see and read the consequences of ignoring any color but the green for go. The trouble was that when NASA went on standby for the count down, it could go on for days or weeks before the space shuttle ever fired its engine. The news presented an immediate dilemma amongst the crew. No fishing, no money, no fun. We ended up waiting around for a couple of days, doings odds and ends to see if the Challenger would make the original countdown. Then NASA changed the date. We realized that this could go on for a long time. So, I called my sister and asked her for a loan. She wired it to me. I told the skipper that I'd come back after the shuttle launched. He agreed. I caught a Greyhound down to West Palm Beach and hooked up with some old buddies of mine. We hadn't seen each other for several years so we went ahead and did the one thing we've always done best, and that was party.

The <u>Challenger</u> was once again was ready to hit the ignition switch. It was January 28, 1986. We were all inside the house drinking and doing lines. While we waited we were watching the television - media coverage was intense. The countdown started, it went to zero. We were all eagerly watching the take off. We watched it climb into the atmosphere on the television. Someone said we would see it better if we went outside. We all ran out into the front yard. It was a cold day by Florida standards. The sky was a light blue with scattered, soft clouds. "There it is," said someone as they pointed.

The shuttle was going up and leaving a massive trail of smoke behind it. Into the atmosphere it went. It was actually only 73 seconds into the <u>Challenger</u> lift off when the NASA spacecraft started to disintegrate. The catastrophe was due to a poor O-ring seal in its right solid rock booster

that failed at lift off. It was as if all of a sudden
there was a fireball, then the formation of a mu-
shroom cloud. It was totally shocking. In awe,
we looked at each other. "Oh My God," were the
words I remembered most from that moment. We
ran back inside to hear the news report. The cam-
eras were following the course of the debris
closely. The replays were painstaking. We had
just witnessed the death of seven brave human be-
ings. It was a tragic but heroic ending. It put a
damper on the good old party feeling.

Nonetheless, it was time for me to return to
Cape Canaveral.

Back at the boat, the jetty was shut down
due to the shuttle recovery efforts. After days
passed, they switched the traffic signal light back
to yellow. I think we had to call for release so we
could get back to home port, which was Fort
Pierce, Florida. It had been a long king mackerel
season with next to nothing to show for it. The
Spanish mackerel run was progressing. We would
venture into the night looking for the phosphorous
to light up the water. We would set and haul back,
picking the Spanish mackerel or pieces of trash fish
from the net. During the entirety of my fishing in
Florida, I've never came across a bail of weed or a
kilo of coke – even though I was always on the
lookout for anything floating. We ended up catching some Spanish mackerel when they started to
run.

Now knowing the run was tapering off, I decided to shove off myself. Alaska rode constant on
my mind. I went and stayed a few days with my
sister. Her husband knew the good ole boys that
owned the swordfish boats and fish hduses. He

took me down and introduced me. Before I knew it, I once again had my sea bag slung over my shoulder, stepping onto my first swordfish boat. The captain, a tall bond-haired, well shaven, was a well-rounded figure of a fellow. He seemed to be an aggressive type of person. My new mate, a short, frizzy haired, dark eyed Portagee looked like he might come out on the winning end of a knife fight. I gave 'em the Alaska spiel. The captain said, "Well, you're not in Alaska anymore." I was thinking that while I knew he was right, I was just on a countdown to get back to Alaska. There, in Alaska, fisherman had a saying, "In Cod We Trust," the Alaska black gold.

We geared up and stowed the groceries away. A small tropical storm had just passed through. The owners of our competitor boats had passed the word - one of their boats hadn't been heard from. He either found the fish or was in trouble. We were to look for all signs of distress. This was a new fishery for me but the lay out was longline snap on. There were flags and bags, buoy depth drops and beacon buoys for locating gear. It seemed different to me being used to gear that's anchored to the bottom. I was excited to see how it was all was going to work. We headed out of the Fort Pierce jetty into a flat, bright and beautiful Atlantic Ocean day. The North Beach was full of bodies lying in the sun. People were walking and wading, splashing in the shallows. The inlet jetties were pretty cool, the people without boats fished from them, watching and waving as the pleasure boats and fishing boats passed by. Dreaming and seeing themselves in a picturesque moment of their most distant fantasies. We always looked back in hope to make it back.

It was later in the afternoon by the time we cleared away from the inner banks of the sandy shores of mainland Florida. We headed northerly into the current of the Gulf Stream. We charged on all through the night. The next morning we were all up together drinking coffee. The Skipper had the Portagee and I start making gear up. The leaders, to be snapped onto the main line, were 36 fathoms long with a big J hook at the end and were wheeled on to a fin-shaped reel. The day went on to pulling out Spanish mackerel and squid to thaw. Taking wheel watches, we were watching the radar closely for solid bleeps that could possibly be our missing competitor boat. Night returned and we were still charging. One of our biggest fears was being run over by super tankers (vessels of massive size hauling foreign cars or products). We cruised through the night doing two-man wheel watches. This was to ensure that the guy at the helm didn't fall asleep and get us run over.

Entering into the light of morning, we got a solid hit on the radar. It was solid and not moving. We set our course in the direction of the bleep. As we got closer and were looking through the binoculars the skipper hollered out, "Looks like we found 'em." As we approached the vessel, there were three men sitting on the stern rail. That was good since that was how many left the dock. The vessel's wheelhouse had been completely ripped from the boat and now faced port and starboard instead of to bow and stern. The skipper got on the single sideband radio, and relayed the longitude and latitude of the competitor vessel. He reported visual vessel damage; also that he could see all three people aboard. As we pulled up, I was looking at the damaged vessel and started to examine the vessel I was standing on. What the fuck kind of fishing had I now gotten myself into?

The Portagee and I got buoys along side the boat, and the tie up lines ready to toss to our ever so anxious and relieved brothers-in-arms. Lines were tossed and the vessels were secured together. The excitement of rescue and the relief of being found after drifting for three days became a clash of smiles, hugs and appreciation on both sides. Only one of the crew had been hurt; a six to eight inch gash on his leg, which they had wrapped and bandaged up nicely. They had been hit with a rogue wave. It took the wheelhouse and all the electronics out with it.

We rolled up several doobies and with a fresh pot of coffee, began to celebrate. With everyone now calmed and settled, we got communications from one of their fleet boats that they had us on radar and would soon arrive to take control and tow the damaged vessel back into Fort Pierce. Within a couple of hours the competitor vessel arrived. We said our good byes and received their gratitude with wishes of a successful swordfish trip. "Cut loose," the captain commanded. As we pulled away, again we looked into each other's eyes, put our hands in the air as if to interweave with one another. It was as if you could feel the power of spirit between us.

It was late afternoon. We headed to God knows where off the Bahamas coast. The Skipper told the Portagee to start getting a set ready. He instructed me on my duties: get the bait out and into the bait trays, light sticks sorted by colors. The light stick is intended to enhance the bait. It is positioned a few fathoms above the bait. The boat slowed, the main line fastened to a beacon buoy. "Let's make a set," the skipper says. The Portagee and I tossed the beacon over and started to pan out the main line. Already instructed on how to thread the mackerel or squid, I had the first bait ready. We were clipping along at about six knots. The Portagee nodded for me to toss the baited leader into the water. First hook. Lights from overhead shining down against the aluminum trays beaming against the light cream of the fiberglass decks and gunnel rails. It felt good. The Portagee though quickly handed me another J hook, taking my second of ecstasy away. I baited the next hook. He played out the leader line and nodded once again for me to throw the bait. There were about three to five hooks per

mile with 26 miles of mainline. A buoy or highflyer flag every mile. There was a beacon buoy on each end with one in the middle in case of parting the main line. The set was made. With the last beacon buoy over now, we waited for tomorrow morning.

While we slept, the 26 miles of fishing gear drifted and worked. Morning came. The skipper poured his coffee, and then went to the direction finder, which tuned into the frequency of our first beacon buoy. We set course by the signal of the direction finder. The skipper had the Portagee and I get some breakfast ready. The beacon signal was weak to start but it got stronger as we downed our coffee and breakfast. With the last cup of morning coffee, we rolled and smoked a fat reefer. The Portagee had filled me with stories of some of his biggest trips with massive sized swordfish, big eye tuna, yellow fin tuna and of course, the massive blue fin tuna. With the signal bar on the direction finder shows full strength, we spotted the buoy. We pulled up with the buoy on our starboard side. The Portagee threw the grapple hook out and snagged the buoy. With the buoy next to the hull, we grabbed it and wrestled it into the boat. The mainline was detached from the buoy and tied back to the main drum. The skipper engaged forward and the mainline drum started to turn. We were hauling gear. I stowed the beacon buoys. As I looked down the gear, I could see buoy after buoy. The first hook came up empty. The skipper unsnapped the hook, and then snapped it down on what was simply called a snap line, which sends the snap of the leader to the stern of the boat so the Portagee can wind it back onto the leader drum. Anxiously, the Portagee and I watch as the next snap came up to the skipper's hand. The skipper hollers out the word "tension," as he started pulling up the leader line - "tension" but not much weight. It didn't matter to me; I just ached to see a fish. The fish hit the surface and with very little effort he flipped a small swordfish up and onto the deck. It excited me - the skipper was not so impressed.

It was time for the Portagee to teach me the job of butcher. The swordfish was dead when it came aboard. The Portagee and I quickly relieved the fish of its head and guts. I scraped the blood-line and trimmed the collar. By the time I got the rat swordfish done, the Portagee handed me a buoy leader to wind up. Watching the skipper and hoping for the word "tension," instead he hollered out, "The buoys are down" which meant something big was on the line! I overheard them talking about how they hoped it wasn't going to be a waste of our time. Sometimes the big fish were a non-sellable fish such as an Atlantic Blue Marlin - those fish could reach well over 1,000 pounds and were equipped with a tapered bill. Hence the name "Marlin Spike." As we eased the main line in, we cleared the leaders and buoys that have been pulled down and finally get to the snap with the weight on it. The skipper said he figured it was dead. In order to get a large fish up we would all take a pull; as one pulled to his fullest, the next person would grab the leader and pull, relieving the other to wait their next turn being equally care-ful not to touch the already stretched monofilament leader to the side of the boat.   With that much tension, the leader could easily snap if it touched any rough surface. Up, up and up we pulled until we could finally see it coming.

It WAS a big swordfish - it was well over 200 pounds - a double marker. That got the ole adrenaline going! We got the gaffs into its head. The skipper grabbed it by the sword. "One, two, three, on the roll," he said. At the roll, the fish came onto the boat. It was massive or at least what I thought of as massive compared to our earlier catch. There were high fives going on right after the sound of the tail slapping the deck. The large swordfish had a kind of a leathery dark skin with a lighter underbelly. It had a stout tapered head, large dark eyes with a large double-edged bill tapered from the center down to the edge. The length depended on size. Its color was kind of an off algae green with rough, sandpaper like surface. The lower jaw extended from behind the eye to the start of the bill, otherwise known as the sword. Swordfish can range from what fisherman call rats, which weigh less than 100 pounds. Once they reach 100 plus pounds, they're gauged in what fishermen call markers.

Alaskan Crude

This fish would have to have its head cut off with the meat saw. It felt great being part of this kind of excitement. Throughout the rest of the day I learned how to clean yellow fin and big eye tuna. When we fought the tuna fish, they taught me that the tuna will burn up its fat content so quickly that it could ruin the price of the fish. Once landed, a live tuna starts beating its tail on the deck at a phenomenal speed, slinging blood everywhere. In order to stop the tuna, a piece of the stiff main line is cut, then snipped to create a cluster of barbs at the end. This device is called a thor. You take the thor and ream it down the vertebrae of the fish and with a solid quick jerk; you pull out the spinal tissue, bringing a quick stop to all resistance. With the various sharks, we would get a tail rap, and then hoist the creature up outside of the boat into the air, de-finning the creature for the fine dining of shark fin soup. After the de-finning, we would cut the creature loose. Thus, the shark would be returned to its natural habitat to be consumed by its fellow comrades.

By the end of the day I had learned to fight swordfish, always being sure that you catch a hold of the sword, not on the upward swing of the fish, but on the down drop. A live large swordfish can definitely hurt a man. I learned how to butcher and bring a tuna from a blood bathing seizure to a dead halt. We had had a decent day of fishing for my first time - it felt phenomenal. Now I no longer feared the thought of the rescue of our competitor boat, I just craved more fish.

After all gear was aboard, the fish packed in ice, we had a meal then prepared to make our second set. While setting the gear, the Portagee started singing some song from the homeland. I couldn't understand what he sang, but it sounded kind of pretty. As the baited mackerel and squid got tossed over, things just started being repetitious, just as fishing usually is. The set was made. We cleaned the deck up, ate, and went to bed. All except one man was on watch for tankers and the like. We would do three-hour shifts.

I awoke in a mesmerized state with my first thoughts being of yesterday followed by the unknown of today. We would do the same as yesterday: coffee, breakfast and a doobie as we traveled towards the end beacon buoy, on course by the direction finder. As we neared the beginning of our string, a call for the vessel ALICIA ANN came over the single sided band. The skipper answered the call. It was the owner of the ALICIA ANN wanting to know if we had started hauling the gear yet, and if so, what we had aboard. The skipper, with a disgusted look on his face, reported that we were just about to start. After they signed off, the skipper started cursing and going on about how many times we would have to stop throughout the day to report to the vessel owner, while he sat at his house figuring out how much to raise the price of the fishing gear, and how much money he was making on the fish we're boarding throughout the day as he sucked down his gin. Then, as he was ranting, I heard that we wouldn't even get paid for the trip we were currently fishing, but for the last trip we brought in. This concerned me. I had always been accustomed to being paid for the trip you brought in at the time. Now, I realize no matter what happens, I'm in for the next trip as well. I might as well fish another trip while I wait for my money. A program that I now know was prearranged to keep the fishermen going back and the owners an upper hand. As the trip continued, I was fighting fish that had nothing but raw energy mixed with a never-ending sense for survival. It subdued all thoughts of my own wants. It was as if I was in a battle with a great adversary and I was charged with conquering its complete domain. Perhaps it was just the butcher in me, meat saw in hand, cutting off my adversaries head!

The Portagee's song from the homeland, night after night, began to work on my nerves. With him being my mentor, I kept my mouth shut. Nearing the end of the trip when we saw buoys down, we started to pray to Oden that what had sunken the gear was the great blue fin tuna to bring in extra booty to our already stowed away bounty which lay below decks iced, awaiting sale. Anytime two blue fins were boarded your trip was over. Two was the legal by-catch limit plus they

were the highest price marketable fish. We did manage to get one before our final string of the trip was set. We also managed to be overtaken ourselves by the United States Coast Guard who ride around in a naval gunner boat. When called to be boarded, our fearless leader, the captain, engaged in another bout of cursing and swearing. I had gotten used to his outbursts, answering the ginned up owner what seemed like 50 times a day. He did go a little extra berserk after answering the Coast Guard back on the VHF (very high frequency) radio. The signal is not as strong as a single side band or the equivalent of what people know as a HAM radio.

The Coast Guard launched from the naval gunner boat. I had been a part of the boarding's in the North Pacific where the Coast Guard showed up in it's own cutter - but this was different. There must have been 200 men standing along the port side of the gunner ship watching as we got boarded. The skipper ranted on about getting fucking boarded every time - you would just think the fuckers would have it figured out by now. "We're just fucking fishermen." As the orange inflatable came alongside the ALICIA ANN, the boarding party wasted no time executing their plan of attack. One right after the other, they come aboard telling us not to move around. It kind of freaked me out. They quickly separated us then we were each put under guard. It was not the most polite boarding that I was used to in the North Pacific, not that you could blame them. It was just like the water in the tropics, you never knew what species of fish you might catch.

The skipper was plenty pissed off and let them know it, especially when they brought out their dope-poking rod. They wanted to shove it down into the fish hold to see what they would come up with. The skipper went nuts. He started right in on the lead officer. "We're just fisherman! If you want a suit against the government then go ahead. The ALICIA ANN gets boarded regularly, you know our homeport, you know where we dock, you also know we're just fucking fishermen. Have somebody watch us unload! However, if you stick that poker down in there...," as they both looked into the opened hatch of the fish hold, "I don't care who buys the fish, the plant or the U.S. government." The officer decided against the probing of the fish hold. He followed the regular procedure of checking for licenses, ID and safety equipment.

Having an Alaska ID has always brought up a few questions. People at that time had no Internet or reality TV shows. They only knew what they might have read in a Jack London story or the place in Nome with a sled dog named Balto. I could tell them that I lived in an igloo and shared a native man's wife to keep warm and they would believe me. All checked out, the orange inflatable was signaled to return alongside. The officer and boarding party now departed back to the gunner ship. We had been thoroughly checked out and our catch still intact. Our personal stash still lay stacked in the stash spot. Those fellows were looking for bigger stuff.

With one last set, we had one more haul before we pointed the boat back to the mainland of Florida. After the haul of the next day, the skipper and Portagee seemed fairly pleased with the trip, stating that it was better than the previous one. Now my thoughts turned to money, alcohol, drugs and women. On the return from the fishing grounds, we traveled back to port with the tide of the Gulf Stream getting us home about twice as fast as getting to the fishing grounds. As we pulled into the plant to unload, the vessel owner was waiting eagerly. The swordfish, tuna, mahi-mahi and shark fins unloaded. The question of money was brought to us. With swordfish price already set, the tuna had to be examined by Japanese buyers for fat content. The tuna would be bid on amongst the Japanese, one by one. The skipper and Portagee receive their pay from the previous trip. The vessel owner, tighter than a frog's ass, didn't even offer me a draw. The skipper, knowing that we were all deserving of at least one good night of getting fucked up, assured me of a draw out of his own pocket as long as I promised to make the next trip. Knowing that I already had planned on it, I gave my word. Just another month or so and I'd be on my way back to Alaska.

Still broke, hoping to have made some money off this trip, I awaited the draw from the skipper. The skipper, the Portagee, and I flew as fast from the boat to the bank as the cockroach flees from the light. Once the money was in hand, a young traveling fisherman could feel as close to a rock star as any other with the hotels, bars, women, fights and lots of buzz, then back to the tour.

So it was the next day, all hung over, that we got pressured from the owner to get right back out there. He showed up with the necessary gear to re-outfit the boat. Getting groceries, ice, and fuel took up the rest of our day. We were ready to set off for another trip. We had one last chance for one last blast. Headed across the tracks to pick up a little blow, then back to the local harbor bar, which kept our asses close to the boat. Later, the next morning, we cut loose into a gloomy, dark day. As we headed back out in to the briny, there was a 25-knot wind chop on top of three-four foot swell; it's not looking too inviting. With no people frolicking around on the south or north beach, there were the hardcore pole fishermen who realize a front coming in could make fishing hopefully better. Once we cleared the outer buoy, the skipper quickly set our course and relinquishes the helm to the protégée and myself. We were on our way for the long charge against the tide and back to the fishing grounds. On this trip the only person I saw was the person who relieved me from watch, so I always saw the Portagee. Once we neared the grounds, it was time to get bait, tie more leaders, and get ready to fish. It was just an hour or so before dark. The skipper told us to get the set ready. Once we were all tied in, we let him know. He told us to throw the beacon buoy and to make a set. The Portagee started singing that same homeland song; we start pulling and baiting, leaders snapping on the mainline. "We're fishing." We pitch the last beacon buoy. Set made.

We cleaned up and the skipper decided we should have a big and decent meal to get started on. As he was getting a loaf of bread or the bag of rice, he started shouting, "Motherfucker, son of a bitch, motherfucker, cock sucker." The Portagee and I looked at each other then back at the skipper. He said, "We got a motherfucker wharf rat." The wharf rat, over our long push to the fishing grounds, had freely foraged through the cupboards. We had pretty much just fed out of the

103

cooler on our way out, saving the mainstay food for the trip.

The first thing that comes to mind is a #3 leg hold trap for catching sable or minks. A wharf rat, if you've ever seen one, can just get quite large. Of course, at this time point, he hadn't had time to graze through all the dry goods. We now would have to constantly check on our food in order to protect it. We had dinner and a doobie. We hit the old fart sack and slept about it. We hoped to have a mega set the following day.

Morning arrived and started as repetitious as the first day of the last trip. As we neared the first end we had high hopes and big dreams. It had stayed dark and yucky with thunderstorms and lightening. The rainsqualls came and went, the ocean choppy. It was a day for full rain gear. We got started and as usual, the owner called first thing through the dark. We hoped to make the trip quick and with lots of profit. The fishing had started out good; if it just held out we could end up with a decent trip. Butchering those big beautiful tuna and swordfish was as if someone had given me a gift like no one else possessed.

We still faced many challenges. I had to put up with the Portagee's never-ending need to sing that same fucking song every night when we set the gear. Each and every fish was a challenge until it hit the deck. It was a challenge not to be run over by a super tanker or freighter. The Coast

Guard had it's own challenges and last, but not least, the smartest motherfucker on the boat was the wharf rat. Who, by the way, was also a mind reader.

About half way through the trip, before I go to bed I think, "Man, those Honey Nut Cheerios would be good in the morning." So I checked the box and it was still fine. The rat must have been thinking the same thing. He would wake up before me and head straight to those Honey Nuts to feed. I can't remember ever wanting to kill something so bad.

The trip went fairly smooth, the sea of the Caribbean calmed back down. The Coast Guard gunner ship boarded us once with an audience of about 200 sailors standing along the gunnel rail. My thought was, "Why don't they give 'em all a tooth brush and put 'em to work?" On a fishing boat you fished, slept or ate; there was always something that needed to be done.

Heading back in to the sandy shores of Florida, we carried a fair payload of product. Thoughts of payment from the previous trip came to mind. I would also have something to compare this trip to, which was a little better than last. With the days on the calendar passing by, I looked forward to Alaska. It would be fun to share my new fishing stories from the Caribbean with my mates of the North Pacific.

Back in town, with the fish unloaded, it was time to get paid. The ginned-up owner cut the checks. It looked way better than the earlier checks from mackerel fishing. This was the beginning of my passage back to Alaska. I called my sister, told her I did good and needed her to hold on to some money for me. "Good idea," was her response. "Which bank are you going to?" she asked, "I'll meet you there." The skipper and Portagee waited anxiously for me to conclude my business with my sister. I hopped back in the car and went straight to a drive through liquor store.

It was time to get our buzz on. Between getting our buzz on and getting ready for our next trip, I met a fellow deckhand off one of our competitor boats. We hung out a bit. I started telling him about Alaska fishing and found out that he had just finished a stint in the Raiford Penitentiary. He started to take a big interest in Alaska. I was no judge so I told him that if he could come up with his grubstake, I would help show him the ropes in Alaska. I also started to explain that I had no trust in the fish house or the owners of the boats. I told him that it would probably be my last trip, so I couldn't get shafted. I would be on my way to Alaska and that's just what they'd think. Even if I did get paid, it wouldn't be a fair shake. Instead of doing a last trip, I found that tickets to Jamaica were cheap. I decided that I was going to take a break from fishing and smoke ganja with the Rastafarians. This penitentiary guy turned "gung ho" right then. He was going to sell his car, stereo set, and whatnot to raise the cash. After making a plan, we sat behind the fish house in his old Chevell smoking reefer and drinking.

Trip three started and all geared up, the cupboards were cleaned of rat damage and rat shit. We hoped that our little furry friend food opponent got lonely for companionship and took flight back into the broken concrete sea walls. The days clicked by on the calendar. With money saved, there was enough left for one trip and one trip to come. I knew I wanted to be back on the West coast early. Sometimes, in order to get on a decent boat, you had to put in a month or so of pretty much free labor. Starting out, it was calm and beautiful. Once again we chugged our way to the fishing grounds. Fishing started with full sized big eye, yellow fin and swordfish. We went back to hand lining - the ultimate of ultimate's. We had set and/or drifted into a school of large mixed fish. If we could continue to get the same drift, hopefully the school of fish would stay abundant and would not travel off too far too fast.

The second day was better than the first. I was butchering swordfish, which ran up to over 300 pounds, the big eye, and yellow fin came in regularly between the Swordfish. The sharks were having a bit of a feed on some of the early bite tuna that fought themselves to death. There was an occasional marlin or sunfish that took the gear down. While hauling it in gently, we wished to see a big blue fin. No matter how gorgeous of a fish, it wasn't always money. We had a really good day of fishing. Once again, just like the night before, the trip before and the trip before that, I listened to the Portagee sing his song. I finally asked him if he had ever heard the song of silence. He just looked at me and kept right on singing. The third morning, the fishhold looked like it did half way through the previous trips. Was the fishing going to hold out? The morning was again dark gray and beginning to get

choppy. We did our usual before coming up on the first beacon buoy. The buoys off of the beacon buoys were sunk. We could only hope it was a blue fin. We got the end, tied it to the mainline and started to haul. Creeping in on the mainline, the skipper got the first hook and passed it back. Whatever it was, it was alive and fighting hard. The skipper had to pan back out the mainline to give the fish something to run on. Finally, he came to the second snap and sent it back. The fish once again took off, needing the mainline to be panned out. The snaps on the mainline were made to slide so a big fish could run, but as in most longline gear, there was a knot. With monofilament, the snap comes tight to the knot; the fish fighting for its life, pulls and tugs so much that the friction burns through the mainline. As the fight contin- ued, the skipper ordered up coffee and a doobie. This was going to take awhile. He panned the gear in and out, driving the boat on it. Finally he got more mainline in than ever and finally here came the third snap hanging heavy on the line. All of a sudden, the snap started popping down the main- line. The skipper, once again, let out line from the drum. We started hauling back in the mainline once again. The snap came once again. It started popping down the mainline. The skipper says, "Fuck, it's sure acting like a big fucking Blue Fin, if not, we're wasting a lot of time," as he panned back out the mainline.

I started thinking, "This is like jaws or some- thing." It gave me an idea - instead of barrels, we should snap a bouy in front of the snap to keep the tension constant and pull on the fish, which in turn would wear the prick out. The skipper agreed.

Alaskan Crude

The next time the snap got close and before the fish took a run, I snapped the buoy on the mainline in front of the leader snap. We were watching the buoy go down, down, down, down in the crystal clear water until it was out of sight. "Better have another cup of coffee and a fatty; this guy is fresh bite, big and still going."

The skipper had a sip of his coffee and started hauling the mainline back in. The Portagee and I watch intently for the buoy. There it was! The Portagee pointed to the buoy rising to the surface. I stood ready with a second buoy to snap on, which I did as soon as I could get it in front of the first buoy snap. Like before, this big fish wasn't coming easy. The snap started popping, the skipper started panning out the mainline - down, down, down went the buoy balls until they were out of sight.

This happened one more time. One more buoy ball now made the count three. One more run for the fish, one more time to pull those buoys down and out of sight. The next time they surfaced, the buoys would lie bobbing in the chop, marking the beginning of what we've been waiting for - a chance to get our hands on the leader. Pull after pull we pull, being extra careful to keep the stretched out monofilament leader away from the hull of the boat. Finally there it was, a great big blue fin. With my heart beating and being a bit panic stricken, the tuna came up. He swam into a circular pattern, which meant that at some point he would be under the boat. It was spooky to see that kind of money fish disappear under the hull of the boat. Nonetheless, we got it to the surface and got the wench hook in it; got it aboard.

It weighed over 700 pounds and it took two and a half hours to fight. We were only on our third hook; it promised to be a very long day. It took the Portagee and I both to relieve our adversary of his head and intestines. As the day carried on, it was another big fish day. I decided to take a few of the swords from the larger fish from the day as proof of my participation in the fishery.

Having the morning mostly taken up by the blue fin brought us towards the end of the set in darkness. Low and behold, the third hook from the end and the gear pulled straight down. We were really excited. With one more blue fin and we could go back to port. This fish wasn't pulling. Was it dead? We got a hold of the leader, and started taking our turns pulling. It was just the Portagee and I doing the pulling. The skipper was jockeying the boat around. We saw it coming out of the shadows of blue. Indeed it was another blue fin and it looked to maybe to be 300-400 pounds. We started cracking comments about going home. The fish was coming up with every stride of arm's length. It started to go into the old tuna turn, circular spin. The skipper decided we should take the leader to the stern of the boat. The Portagee moved around the leader drum, which blocked a clear path to the stern. I went to pass the leader to the Portagee, the fish now near the surface. We were all thinking, "We got this fucker, we're going home." Instead, the Portagee and I fuck it up by letting the leader touch the side of the rail where a screw head lay exposed, cutting the leader like butter. Our hearts hit the deck as we watched our ticket home sink back into the blue darkness to become a delicious dinner for that prehistoric creature, the shark.

The ranting started. Our skipper pissed the fuck off, stomping and jumping and yelling, headed back to the hauling station. Grabbing the broken leader snap, he cussed up a storm. We had counted the fish as good as on the boat, only to make the tragic mistake. The skipper started to haul the rest of the gear. It was later than normal, and instead of pointing to port, we started to get ready for another set. Then we received a call from the Coast Guard. We should prepare to be boarded. The skipper, already frustrated to maximum, hung the mic up. "Fuck, we've got to get back to our location for setting; if they want to board us, they can do it underway."

The Navy gunner must have thought "They're running," and the smoke came out of their engine stacks. The skipper throttled down, pointed the vessel to the set location. It wasn't much longer when the orange inflatable came alongside, bashing along the choppy seas. As the inflatable rises on the swell, one man rolled out and onto the boat. He demanded that we stand still; another man on the boat on the next swell, and so on and so on until there were five. They weren't in a good mood and neither was the skipper. They wanted to know why we didn't cease and desist. The skipper started accusing them of hindering our right in the pursuit of happiness, which for us, was to fish. We went

through the whole ordeal once more; we had no
drugs or violations that were found.

We made the set, and went to bed disgusted
with the thought of my part of the fuck up. The
next day listening to the a.m. radio, Paul Harvey
came on. He went into the largest cities in the U.S.
He said that with a population of 3500, Sitka,
Alaska was the largest city. The landmass surrounding the city was counted as city. This didn't
include the amount of land surrounding the bottom
of the island and the city of Port Alexander. Most of
Baronof Island is mountains and is uninhabitable,
yet enchanting. All of the forest was included as
the City and Borough of Sitka.

Hearing this made me reflect back on my
friends and the fishing in Alaska. It was time to let
the skipper know that I wouldn't be making another trip with him. As I announced my intentions, the
skipper's only reply was, "A fellow has to do what a
fellow has to do. Just keep hauling the gear." The
Portagee and I pretty much just kept our heads
down and our mouths shut through the day. Not
only was morale low, the fishing had fallen off.
With a nice payload already aboard, we fished out
the remaining days. We cleaned and iced and
thought that it had turned into a really nice trip. If
we had gone in early, we would have missed out
on value of the end product, which was far over
the last trip now that we had a blue fin.

While I appreciated falling into the sword
fishing, I was now plotting my way to return to the
northwest. It was a good thing that the fishing
supplied me with enough money to get back, but
also to take a break from fishing - to go on a roll.

Alaskan Crude

With the boat unloaded, cleaned, and checks handed out, I ran into my buddy Mr. Ho off of the competition vessel. Mr. Ho was still ready to sell everything and quit the vessel if I was still going to Jamaica. With check in hand, I said that I would check on the arrangements. Then, just as in a dream, I found myself stepping off of a Greyhound, flagging a checkered cab down with Mr. Ho by my side.

Once in the back of the cab, the driver asked what we were in town for. We let him know that were sword fishermen on a party break before we headed to the Alaska fishing grounds. "And by the way," I said, "Do you know where we could pick up a little blow?" He let us know that he could help with any need, which he did, and then he took us to a fancier hotel than that which we had in mind. I thought, "What the hell, we are on a roll." So we let it be.

The night went by and so did the coke and the alcohol in the mini bar. By the time daylight revealed itself we were fucked up. Splashing down in the shower, I did a line and a drink. We paid the tab and grabbed a cab to the airport. I couldn't really remember the state of the play at the airport though I do remember sitting on the plane and looking down over Cuba thinking of Fidel Castro sucking and fondling that fat Cuban cigar while commanding his troops. The next thing I knew, the stewardess was shaking me awake. Mr. Ho and I were the only ones left on the plane. Mr. Ho was still passed out in the aisle seat next to me. The stewardess was shaking him to no avail. She looked at me and pointed for me to get Mr. Ho up and off of the plane. With a few good elbows into

Mr. Ho's solar plexus, his eyes popped open and he realized, as I did, that we were the last people left on the plane and that we definitely needed to get the fuck off.

After getting that much needed nap, we stepped out into the bright sunlight. Like a couple of vampires, we scurried from the beams of ultra-violet into the terminal to collect what little attire we traveled with. Passing thought the terminal doors and stepping out into the tropical environment of Jamaica, we were immediately surrounded by offers of weed. We were standing in front of the Jamaican military armed with M16s, who were there to protect the security of the terminal. Unreal! They didn't seem to give a shit about a fellow islander doing a little business. "I know what you're here for," echoed from more than one man's mouth.

Ignoring the onslaught of salesmen, I motioned for a cab. We had landed down in Montego Bay. I had prearranged a hotel through the travel agency. The Jamaican cab driver, after getting the name of the hotel, began his sales pitch with enthusiasm. As we pulled up to the plush hotel, I noticed the beautiful vegetation growth running rampant, following its own course of life. I looked at the cab driver and asked how much it was if I paid in American. The driver informed me that I could get a better exchange rate if I dealt with the Rastafarian in the street or shops in the town rather than with the local banks. I thanked him for the tip.

There was a young teenage boy standing eagerly by to take our packs and introduce us to the main lobby, then to our room. There was a small air conditioner in the window, wood slated blinds, two heavy-duty cot bunks, and one large ceiling fan. In the bathroom there was ceramic tile all around and a light bulb with a drawstring. There was a shower, a shitter, and a well-used sink stained by sulfur water over the years.

I pitched my stuff onto one of the bunks. Mr. Ho did the same. We changed into our shorts and went out to the pool. There were lounge chairs and umbrella tables with chairs surrounding a porcelain blue green pool, done up in local stone for a tropical experience. We grabbed a couple of lounge lizard foldouts and with our new and young companion hot on our heels and eager to please, we ordered up a couple of drinks. Basking in the sun, drinks headed in our direction, it was time to score a little weed. With the delivery of our chosen beverage, I gently ask if he could score us a little weed. He simply smiles and says, "No problem." I handed him a ten. He was back in ten minutes or so, very quick. He motioned from the arched rock entrance to the pool area for me to come over. We stepped around the corner of the building. The reached down and under a bush pulled out a brown paper grocery sack half fucking full of nice Jamaican ganja. The only problem was that it was way more than I wanted. I reached into the bag, got a handful to show the kid and said that was all I needed. "You keep the rest, but I want you to roll me up some joints. When I order a

drink I'll get a couple. Can you handle that?" Same as before, the answer was, "No problem."

Mr. Ho and I decided to go downtown and check it out. Ther were all kinds of shops selling various things. The Rastafarian wood carvings caught my eye, as did the beautiful Jamaican girls. Picking up a local smoking pipe, I traded my U.S. dollars for Jamaican money. I got a better rate. I had mentioned to one of the local vendors that I was hoping to get some homemade rum. No problem once again was in the answer. He directed me to a little shanty no bigger than a couple of pieces of plywood with a corrugated tin roof. Inside stood a couple of old wooden chairs and a rickety little table with a small made up bar. Behind the bar stood a little and very wrinkled old lady. I asked politely for some rum, and put some money on the bar. She poured me a shot. It went down smooth and was clearer than clear. I could tell after a taste that I was about to become magnified. I smiled at her and with her yellow, stained teeth she smiled back sweetly.

There were rows of old Pepsi bottle behind her that she used to sell rum to go. I had her fill one for me and took another shot. I thanked her. She looked at me in not such a friendly way and said, "Don't lose your bottle boy or you get no more here." Containers were tough to come by. Each day I would fill up my bottle and then return it to her on my way out of town. Ho was doing his own thing. We partied around the villa and then split up.

I thought it was time to move to Negril where I had already arranged to stay at the Rock House. Before heading out of Montego Bay, Ho and

Alaskan Crude

I heard about a place to rent some little Honda 125mph motorcycles. We checked it out, and made a deal with the Jamaican using the barter process. Ho asked me if I could carry his part until we got back and got paid off of the last swordfish trip. I was still fairly pat so I agreed.

Now we were feeling like two cool dudes as we rolled into Negril. With our buzz on, shirts off, packs strapped to the back of our steeds, we moved through town and pulled over to ask for directions to the Rock House. The Rock House Villas lay above the rocky cliffs of Jamaica. They dropped off into the blue of the Caribbean waters. There were caves to explore and water to snorkel, and a nice ladder to climb back up the rocky cliffs. The villa had slat wood framing with a palm frond roof. Inside, two midsize regular beds, a ceiling ban, a stand up shower, and pretty much the same layout inside as the other place, just a lot nicer. The place was cool.

We got situated and then took a header off of our front cliff balcony. Back on top, it was time to get something to eat and to cruise the boulevard. Across the street was a small local café where the pork was freshly killed and the marijuana bread was freshly baked and served with goat cheese. A nice little body high. Ho and I took up residence at night in the nearby outdoors resort bar.

During the day we rode our cycles and swam in the crystal blue waters. One day, when I pulled up to a stop signed, I looked over at the locals sitting on a concrete wall. A beautiful Jamaican girl asked if she could go with me. I replied, "Hop on." She did. She was built like a brick shit house. She wrapped her arms around me and off we went.

Needless to say, it didn't take long and we were naked in the bungalow. She was as fine as silk. With no contraception, we banged along like a couple of wild animals. I've often wondered since if I don't have some Jamaican offspring kicking around somewhere.

Time was growing short and so were my pockets. Ho was hitting me up regularly for money, playing backgammon against the Jamaicans, or the prostitutes were getting him for all of his worth. With no more money left to loan, I started to worry about surviving our last few days. At night I would venture into the back of the resort to an area restricted to natives only. The shanty shacks had an open fire with a large kettle of fish soup bubbling away. A couple of big Rastas asked me if I knew that I was in the wrong area. So, to break the ice, I asked if I could get a taste of their authentic food. A large woman stirred the kettle of fish soup. She reached for a paper bowl and picked out some kind of green looking grass. She looked at me and said, "This is just for flavor. If you eat it, it will make you sick." She handed me the bowl and a plastic spoon. It was the most delicious soup I had ever tasted. I had to ask for seconds. After the meal I offered a couple of bucks, which they gladly accepted. One of the Rastas had a spliff burning and offered it to me. We sat and talked of their country, politics, cane sugar, tourism, and the politics of gunrunners and dope smugglers. It seemed the two politicians had two different views of the country needs. Voting day was approaching and I was warned that it would be best to stay inside until elections were over.

Alaskan Crude

With just a couple of days left and just a couple of bucks, I had the possibility of starving due to that fucking Ho. At that point, we were not getting along. I let him know that he was on his own. I ventured over to the little restaurant where I had gotten most of my morning meals and let the owner lady know about my dilemma. She went into the kitchen and returned with a loaf of pot bread and a large chunk of goat cheese. I gave her what little cash I had left. That food was going to have to last two days before I could get on the plane back to Miami.

The two days passed with me seeing very little of Ho until the morning we caught the bird out. Ho showed up to get his shit with four scratches down his face. He had been with a prostitute and had no money. I just looked at him and said, "Doesn't look to me like that was the pussy cat's first scratch." He just rolled his eyes and dropped his head and went in to get his stuff.

We got a concierge ride to the airport. Hungry, broke, and ready to dump Ho, I got to the ticket counter thinking of the little package of nuts we would get on the plane. I handed the gal at the counter our tickets. She said everything looked good but that it would be $40. I looked at her as I almost shit myself and said, "What? We already paid for the tickets."

"Yes but you haven't paid your exit visa tax. Don't you have a credit card?"

"I can assure you that I have no money and I don't have a credit card," I replied.

"It's either the money or the immigration man's office."

Alaskan Crude

I felt like I was in a Crosby, Stills, Nash, and Young song, "Mr. Immigration Man please just let me get through." The immigration man was a big man dressed in government clothing. He was well manicured and wore a belt with a pistol attached to it. On his chest was a badge, shiny as a new penny. We walked up to his office and he motioned for us to come in. He noticed Ho's scratches right off and then he looked at me. I explained the situation while he stared directly into my eyes. Once again, the question of credit cards came up. It was as if all tourists had them. The problem was, I explained, that we were just traveling sword fishermen, not your everyday common tourist. "From the looks of you, I would have to agree," the immigration guy replied.

"It wouldn't be good for us to not be able to go home," I said. "We'll probably end up in the local jail from trying to catch a boat out of here." He actually chuckled, then said, "Alright, I let you guys go, but next time think about bringing a credit card." I was thinking that since Ho was into me for several hundred dollars, the thought of near starvation could have all been avoided if I would have just said "no" to Ho.

Finally on the plane back to Miami, I proceeded to rim Ho a new asshole. We were going to be thumbing back north if we didn't get some money. "I'll call my mom, Charlie," was his reply. Down on the ground and in the main terminal, Ho made a collect call to his mother and convinced her to wire us a couple hundred bucks Western Union. We received it shortly. Ho split it with me and we grabbed some grub before heading to the Greyhound station. I explained to Ho that I'd be

120

stopping off in West Palm Beach and there was no place for him where I was going. I'd catch back up with him in Ft. Pierce when I came to collect the last of my pay. Then off to Alaska we would go.

As the Greyhound pulled into the West Palm Beach Terminal, I looked at Ho as he scratched a starting scab on his face. "I'll meet you in Ft. Pierce. The next few days I will spend with family and friends. Some of my family floated me a little cash. I have to catch the plane to Alaska out of West Palm Beach anyways."

So I had a little more fun in the sun before returning to collect my pay. Once I got back to Ft. Pierce, I stayed at my sister's. She drove me down to the little fish plant to get my check. Of course she knew all the main old boys down at the plant through her husband. I collected my check and asked if they had seen Ho. They informed me that Ho caught a swordfish boat out yesterday. The fucker, I knew he was going to try to avoid me. I asked if by chance he had left any money for me. "No," was the reply. I thanked them for the job and we left.

I let my sister know that the fucker was try-ing to rip me off and that we should speak to her husband. He, in turn, could talk to his buddies down at the plant and she could keep any money they got out of Ho.

I had to get back to the great Northwest be-fore any collection of debt would occur. A couple of days later, sitting on the big bird to Seattle, I thought of how Ho was going feel having his mon-ey taken from him when he got back to the dock. I smiled as I thought of the prosperous new season ahead of me in the Gulf of Alaska.

Alaskan Crude

7

MISSION IMPOSSIBLE

The sea cucumber industry started up in the late 1980s. At the time I had a little 33 foot double ender named the CAROL L. A sea cucumber is an ocean going worm that feeds on vegetation. It has a leathery back with a softer underside; it's hard to tell the asshole from the head. It is sliced down the middle and scraped with a wide putty knife for the strips of muscle meat. The body is then dried and processed for sea food flavoring. The fishery starts in the mid fall and runs through mid winter when the weather and temperature of the water can come to their coldest temps.

My friend Scotty, an ex submarine Navy man and diver, convinced me to rig the CAROL L. for cucumber diving. Scotty, tall and of Swedish heritage, started to gather the dive gear. Personally I had no dive gear and very little experience except snorkeling off the Florida Keys for lobster.

We started gathering air compressors, hose, and building bags to put the cucks in. We had a theory of how it would all work. It started out with us drinking in the P Bar. Everyone was listening to us "rave on". Rita, the bartender said, "Oh boy, here goes mission impossible again." That got a laugh from everyone. Usually whatever mission Scotty and I started on eventually became impossible for us to finish.

We didn't have much room on the CAROL L. and there would be three of us, plus gear for two divers. Scotty said, "Oh no Charlie, you're going down, learn to be a harvester not a sightseer." So it began. He bummed me a dry suit designed for a tall Swede instead of a small Irish German. He got me fins and headgear. He said, "It's the only suit we got so we'll make it work." I didn't get any of the fancy gear like a depth gauge. We hired Ray as our cuke tender and loaded the compressor, hose, and storage gear for the cucks. We devised a plan of cleaning the sea cucumbers under the water as we picked or harvested them. Ray would haul the bags of cleaned sea cukes aboard using the jerry-rigged picking boom. We would load the bodies into five gallon buckets lined with Visquene bags, then the buckets of product would be put down into the fish hold and iced. It all sounded good when we theorized it at the P Bar.

The day before opening, we headed out for Goddard Hot Springs, just a couple hours to the south of Sitka. We were to make our first jump in Dorothy Narrows. Scotty started to give me my emergency training course verbally, as we made our way to the hot springs. "If this happens to you, you've got to do this or you'll die." Every few words would include, "Do this or you'll die." I was getting the naval dive-training course 101 on the way to the grounds. By the time we arrived at Goddard Hot Springs, I had been filled with what to do if tragedy struck or otherwise. I was to not fuck around, pick sea cucumbers as fast as possible, and to only see sea cucumbers. Once again, Scotty reminded me, "You're a harvester, not a sport diver." At that point I was thinking that I had only just tried the oversized dive suit on and had never even got wet in it.

Opening day came with a morning of smoke on the water showing us that the temperature was down. Still, it was clear and calm. In the winter months the visibility of the water is much better than in the summer due to the lack of plankton blooms. We dropped anchor at the mouth of Dorothy Narrows. We coffeed up, puffed up, and started to gear up using the buddy system. Ray started the air compressor. Scotty and I suited up as I received some last minute reminders.

It was time to put the weight belts on and get in the water. Scotty tightened up on my weight belt straps. He cinched his. Off the stern we went. I bobbed like a cork; the oversized suit had a big air bubble up behind my neck. The bubble was higher than my release valve on the top of my left arm shoulder. Every time I tried to go down, I couldn't force myself hard enough - the air pocket forced me right back to the surface. Scotty, of course, was watching, waiting, instructing me and laughing his ass off. Rolling from side to side, I tried to get the trapped air vented out. The humor and impatience wore on Scotty. Finally he said, "I'm going down before I piss in my suit." He disappeared with a deft quickness.

Still struggling and cussing, I thought that if I could just get down the air bubble would compress due to the atmospheric pressure. The deeper you go, the more the molecules are compressed - Scotty Naval Training 101. So it came to me: there was an anchor on the bottom and gear going to it. I swam to the anchor line and started pulling and kicking my way down. It worked and I was going down. The air compressor must have been working double time. The deeper I got, the easier things got and the more relaxed I got. About this time I reached the anchor. I felt a tug on my leg that scared the shit out of me. My first thought was that it was a sea lion. I turned to look and found it was Scotty. He had filled his first bag, and then came to check on me. He was all thumbs-up. He smiled and pointed down to the bottom. He showed me his cuke bag and swam off.

Back on my own, I slowed my breathing down, relaxed for a moment and took in the awesome surroundings. Then I saw one - it was time to be a harvester. They lay on and along the big-eared kelp. I reached down, picked my first sea cucumber. I took the small, extremely sharp little curved Victornox knife and gutted my first sea cucumber, and stuck it in the bag. It felt good. I grabbed another one, lifted and looked through the kelp; it was pretty good picking.

The tidal waters in Alaska are quite large, making the current run fast and hard. Most divers swim with the current when harvesting. With us being anchored, I finally came to the end of the distance with the air hose. My bag nearly full, I surfaced. Trying to swim into the current while towing several hundred pounds, I was exhausted. I called for Ray to pull me in by hose, by hand. I still swam as diligently as possible. Upon getting to the boat, Ray got the bag of cukes on board, and helped me on board. It was time for a cup of coffee and a breather.

Scotty showed up minutes later. Ray hooked the bag of cucumbers up; we hoisted the bag aboard, pulled the drawstring - the cucumbers spelled onto the hatch. Scotty handed me his weight belt, pulled himself aboard. We looked at each other, smiled and chuckled. Ray commenced to fill the lined five gallon buckets with cucumbers. Scott and I oversee the product quality. The five gallon buckets were stored in the fish hold side by side with ice between the buckets. Satisfied, we were on our way to prosperity.

We got a coffee, a doobie, and our minds right. Back to the program. With weight belts back on, air compressor on, Scotty reminded me that I'm a harvester and then disappeared under the surface. I looked at Ray, put my ass on the rail, mask down, breathing apparatus in, I splashed down. My suit still compressed, I had to struggle to get down, but at least the anchor line wasn't needed. Back on bottom, the current was running harder than before. If you harvest with the current you can silt up the area making it difficult to see the product. Nevertheless, you keep at it, swimming into it. Still being carried back.

I was getting some cucumbers, and starting to feel good about being a harvester. The small curved Victorinox had somehow slipped off my wrist. I reached to pick it up, rolled over on my back so the band would go down my wrist. Unexpectedly, I started rocketing to the surface. My heart fell to the bottom while my body headed the other way. The first thing in my mind was Scotty 101. What the fuck did he say? About that time my mouth regulator piece was ripped out from my mouth. I was in trouble. It was a good thing Scotty was a good teacher. The animation with instruction helped his words stick in my head, especially the part about "Do this or you're gonna die." So it came to me. Spread your arms and legs and exhale. Rocketing to the surface I just prayed not to have embolize. I hit the surface, popped up, and caused a wake to rock the CAROL L. I was so happy to still be alive, looked for the boat. I could see Ray looking back at me. I swam to the boat breathing heavy, shaking. Arriving, Ray helped me in. "What the fuck happened?" he asked. I explained the loss of my weight belt. Ray pulled the hookah system or air line with the regulator and weight belt back to the boat, while I sat there and shook. Ray, concerned for me, asked, "You think this diving is for you?"

Alaskan Crude

"All I know is it must be like being bucked off a horse, if I don't go again right now, I'll never know because I'll never go again." I reached my hand out. Ray, fairly reluctant to pass the hookah system, said, "Fuck man, I hope you know what you're doing." I know he could see the fear in my eyes as I slid off the side of the boat.

Back down on the bottom, I was nervous but I knew shit happens and it just happened to me. 101 got me through it. I found a nice band of cucumbers laying on the edge before the drop off to the deep. I started to harvest and got back in my own, losing the fear. As I picked, I kept running these words through my mind. "I got my mind on my money, my money on my mind." My bag was filling up. Suddenly I noticed I was having a problem trying to get oxygen out of my regulator. I held my mind on "My money, and my money on my mind". The cuking was good. I figured Ray must have let the air compressor run out of gas. But he would be quick, knowing we were down and working. Looking towards the surface, the sun was slicing down. I went from one full pull of oxygen to half a pull to a quarter pull, to no pull. Ray was not going to make it in time. I had waited far too much time. I dropped my bag and started to swim breathlessly up. With no depth gauge, I pressed towards the rays of sun. The brighter they got the closer I was. By the time I reached the surface, I felt I had used every air molecule and muscle in my body. Once again I was just glad to be alive. Scotty was already on the boat with Ray. Once again I was hauled to the boat by the hookah hose. Pulled aboard, shaking like a leaf, I started to bitch about the air but I could hardly get any cuss words

129

out. Scotty said, "If you wouldn't have panicked, the molecules in the hose were expanding half way up, you could have got a hit of air from the hose itself." It wasn't the gas, the compressor crapped out. We returned to town with fresh new product, which equaled wages. Except for me, as far as I was concerned my life was wages enough.

The cucumber industry turned limited entry. If you participated and produced poundage, you earned the right to be one of the few to harvest today or sell out your right to the fishery. I decided to stay topside with the vessel, being captain, cook, and cuke cleaner.

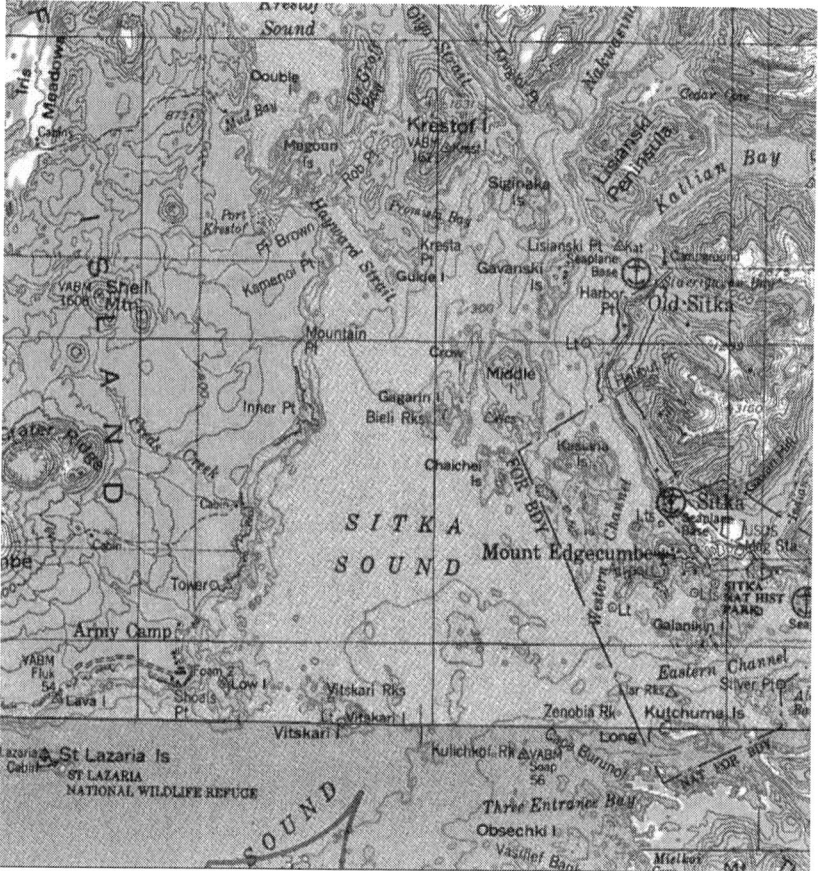

"HYDRO"

8

"HYDRO"

Some people come to Alaska to break trail, set
way, find prosperity or raise a family with one's
own morals. Others are leaving the past or wanting no part of their inevitable future. One sunny
summer afternoon while sitting on the end bars-
tool, half tattered up; I was trading sea stories
with my fellow patron when I felt a hand on my left
shoulder. Turning my head, I looked up the tat-
tooed arm and into the eyes of my good friend,
Shiner. At the time Shiner was a fisherman by
trade, and a tattoo artist by profession. Shiner
said, "Charlie, hey man, I want to introduce you to
Rich, a friend of mine. He just got out and flew up
here to check it out." My eyes rolled over to Rich.
The fellow stood about my height, had heavy
brown skin, white t-shirt, and blue jeans with
sneakers. His long ass hair was pulled in a tight
ponytail, and covered in jailhouse tattoos. He was
thicker than three of me. His forearms were the
size of my biceps, biceps the size of my thigh. He
put his hand out. I looked back at Shiner and said,
"Get this mother fucker away from me. There's
only one way they let him out and that's so he can
narc people off." Shiner, surprised, but not that
surprised, quickly put his hand on Rich's shoulder.
Rich was tense, looking at Shiner. Shiner said,

"It's all right man," to Rich. "Charlie's all fucked up, let's just go." I turned my head and went right back to ranting and raving about our sea stories and our abilities.

At the time I was a troll deckhand out of the ANB harbor and was working for Paul on the fishing vessel PERIL STRAIT. Paul, all Alaskan, was one of the easiest going men I had ever fished with. With a ball cap, jean jacket, Levi denim pants and rubber boots, Paul was an electrical lineman by occupation, fisherman by trade. His Chesapeake retriever "Toes" was always faithfully by his side. The PERIL STRAIT, a 36-foot gillnet style vessel was hand built in 1967 by Harry Jimmy, a native man of culture and many talents.

One of the common fisherman superstitions is to not go to sea with money in your pocket because that may be all you return with. You should throw even your change into the ocean. My take on the matter is if you leave broke, any thing you come back with is better.

I took this to heart back then. I was planning on spending every last dime on that bar stool. In the morning when the engine started, I came to with flat pockets and a throbbing head, feeling like a hung over sailor ready for the revitalization and cleansing of the sea. It was like when I was a child and my parents would take us kids to the beach. We would wash away and cleanse our scrapes and sores while we played, never knowing the difference. The oceans have many healing powers.

We cut the lines and ties from all. Dropped the trolling poles. It was Silver salmon or Coho season only. We headed south through the mink trail, a maze of small islands, reefs and rock piles.

The route is protected from the ocean swell. We passed Frosty Reef, Goddard Hot Springs, and went into Dorothy Narrows. We came out and turned into Windy Pass, full of bays to the Baranof side. Ocean islands to the sea side. Salmon streams, brown bear, Sitka blacktail deer, mink, martin, land otter and sea otter. At the tops, the mountain goat, safe on the ridges and gorges impossible to get to in their kingdom. In this land you're a guest of nature not the predator. It may let you take from it, but alone in the woods, out of bullets, more than likely you will be consumed.

The south side of Windy Pass leads into Crawfish Inlet; the inlet a deep trench that penetrates deep into Baranof Island. It also leads the way to the open waters of the Gulf of Alaska. We headed out to the 50 fathom edge to drop the gear in. In the troll pit, while sharpening hooks, I noticed sea scooters or fish ducks. They were so full of bait or feed they could hardly paddle out of the way of the boat. Good sign. So fat they couldn't fly. Paul slowed the boat to trolling speed, engaged the hydraulics. Gave me the word to put the gear in. He pointed the PERIL STRAIT towards Whale Bay. Once all four lines were out and the gear completely deployed, the springs or indicators of fish on, started to jerk. Paul came to the wheelhouse door, "Looks like we got wiggles. Give it a couple minutes, then haul 'em." "Right on" I replied. I Reached inside my rain gear down into my pants pocket, and got a hold of my deer horn pipe and weed. Loaded a bowl, squatted down in the troll pit. Got me a few good green hits. Time to haul the gear. Silver salmon, during the early part of the season, are an average of 4 and a half to 5 and a half pounds each.   Right after you've been pulling King salmon that average 18 to 20 pounds, these fish appear tiny. Now, we had to release those big money fish while knowing that our trip check was going to be as small as the fish we were catching.

The further south we went, I noticed the sea birds building in numbers. The scooters, now by the hundreds, spread over the sea. Off in the distance I could see pods of whales expelling their massive lungs full of oxygen against the while clouds and multi blue sky. As I looked into the mountains of mist, one breached, coming out of the water like a nuclear missile being fired from a submarine. Then gravity overcame the missile. The missile slammed back into the sea, exploding with massive force. The ocean rose into the sky, and then fell back into its own dimension once more.

The breeching whale actually has an itch it can't scratch. The barnacles have grown so thick that the whale slams itself in to the sea to knock them loose and get relief. Once it has a foothold, the barnacle set out to open up the biggest orgy house in the available area. Being one of the fastest multiplying creatures in the ocean, they open their shell body, stick their dick neck out, and poke any and all others it can around it. The one next to that one is trying to fuck everything in its reach and on and on, causing one of the biggest releases of organism growth imaginable. Late in the evening, we headed into Still Harbor, the most outer anchorage, in the mouth of Whale Bay to the south side. Paul pulled the PERIL STRAIT in amongst the trollers already at anchor. With the anchor dropped and secured, we cleaned the deck, iced fish, and hit the rack.

For the next few days, we fished out of Whale Bay. Paul decided to head to the end of the island to sell to the ALASKA QUEEN, a buying scow located in a small township named Port Alexander. The ALASKA QUEEN, a floating barge had an ice-maker, washing machines, showers, and small store with food and fishing gear. The QUEEN bought fish for one of the local fish buying plants in Sitka. The fish was iced and loaded into insulated totes to be later picked up by the tender EYAK. It would then be taken back to Sitka to the processing plant, a 10 to 12 hour trip straight through. If the tender wasn't full, he would call out on the marine radio to fishing vessels, and stop in the various bays to buy fish and re -ice boats.

Port Alexander, a whaling station and herring reduction plant back in the early 1900s, was once a vibrant fisheries community. With the whaling industry over and the herring reduction plants shut down due to over fishing of the herring, the town survived because of the salmon fishery. In the 1920's, Port Alexander was one of the world's largest King salmon producers. The once robust town caught fire and burned; taking the fish canneries, supply stores and most of the homes with it. The township was part of the City and Borough of Sitka. Later in 1974, the people of Port Alexander gathered a committee together of people who had different city values from the people of Sitka and seceded from the City and Borough of Sitka.

We unloaded our catch and got cleaned up. One nice little bonus was that the processing plant would send down cases of beer by the pallet loads. On a decent trip, they would toss a case to the boat. Over to the tie up float we went. I had put money on a small piece of beachfront land and already had many friends living in P.A. I watched my buddies and their families float drums of fuel over to the beach, roll them by hand to their houses. They pushed wheelbarrow loads of groceries and supplies on slash boards through the soft wet muskeg trails. They kept generators running because the only electricity service was the service you provided. No fish plant, no ice machine, and no supply store. I ended up telling the guy to just keep my down payment money.

Port Alexander, it could be said, was the town of broken dreams. Some thought of it as their own Shangri la. Others spent a winter and now understood what the saying "hell freezes over" is all about. Spring and summer, you could swim, there's no place more beautiful. Fall and winter, be prepared for no communication, water to freeze for an undetermined amount of time, and to be self-sufficient. You never leave home without a flashlight. When it gets dark, it is blacker than Aunt Jemima's ass. It's a town of boardwalks, not roads. Transportation is running a skiff or oaring a rowboat.

Over to the tie up float we went. Once lashed securely to the boards, Paul shut down the boat. I had already iced the beer. The dock had groups of people sitting on the bull rails, plastic lawn chairs, and five gallon buckets of iced beer. Barbecues smoked. There were smiling faces, hugs and handshakes as we made our way from one end to the other. Everyone passed you a beer or joint.

Sitting there, bullshitting about and admiring the different vessels, someone pointed out a 36-foot 1918 horseshoe stern little troller named THE ESTHER to me and said, "The guy that fishes it is quitting fishing and is just going to leave the boat tied to the dock." They also informed me that the fish plant in Sitka, Sitka Sound Seafood, held the note on the boat. Back in the day if the plant believed in your ability as a fisherman, they would

help get you started either with a fishing permit or boat. Just like standing in the cross road or working for the coal mine, when you signed the contract you just as well signed in blood. When you brought in your catch, 30 percent would be taken back as payment. Usually it was enough to keep you borrowing until your next endeavor.

Alaskan Crude

I found the fellow who ran the ESTHER. He told me it was a fact that he was quitting and leaving the boat, which would more than likely eventually end up in the back bay alongside the other vessels in the boat graveyard. I already had my signature on a contract from a previous dealing with my first salmon hand troll permit. I called the plant manager, explained the situation with the vessel. I told him I had a $1,000.00 for down payment. The manager told me he would ask the boss and would let me know within the hour. It wasn't 15 minutes later when I received the message: "Tell Charlie to get the keys, they're his."

So, once again, I find the now ex skipper of the ESTHER. He had no problem relinquishing the keys to me. With a huge smile on my face, the vessel keys in my hand, I am now once again a captain of my own vessel. The down side was I had to let Paul know he was out a deck hand. As I entered the PERIL STRAIT, half drunk from celebrating my new command, I sat down at the galley table. I looked over at Paul and then dropped the hammer. "Paul, you're now looking at the captain of the ESTHER." Paul congratulated me, asked me what I was going to do with the ESTHER seeing as to how I have no salmon fishing permit. I told him the plant kicked me down a boat, hopefully they would eventually help out with a hand troll permit. I offered to go ahead and fish a trip back to town, then fly back to Port Alexander. There were two scheduled flights a week on a 180 Cessna or Beaver float plane. Port Alexander was accessible by boat or float plane. Paul, knowing that was not really what was in my heart, said, "No, that's alright, you better stay here with your new boat." We had a few beers and I packed my shit and moved over to the ESTHER.

In the morning when I got up, Paul was gone. My life now was an unexpected whirlwind. I was a boat owner without a permit. I looked across the float over to L.J.'s troller live aboard. L.J., a long time Alaskan fisherman party animal and his girl friend, Princess Comotos lived on it. As a true Indian princess, alcohol took the best of. L.J. and the Princess. Already awake and pissing over the rail, L.J. saw me and said, "Hey, Charlie, ready for a beer and puff?" I waved my hand, said, "I'll be right over in a minute." I slid over and put my ass on the bull rail. L.J. handed me a beer and pipe. The harbor, empty of all working boats, was left only with broken engines boats or people without salmon permits. As I peered down the end of the dock, I saw someone rolling out of a punt. Headed down towards us came that fucking Rich that Shiner introduced me to. It looked like he was carrying a fifth of cheap rotgut. He showed up talking some drunken shit, handed off the bottle of rotgut to L.J.   I swilled my beer and told L.J. "See ya later. I'm going to mess around on the ESTHER."

There wasn't any supply of alcohol in town. Even though it was a dry town, it had some of the wettest lips around. It seemed Rich had about a half of case of those rotgut bottles. He was squatting in a small cabin decorated in animal skulls, bones and horns: The death wall. He also had the wall of wanted convicts. Wanted posters were lined up side by side until they covered the small cabin wall. A little while passed by and I saw the three of them load up in the punt and disappear to the other side of the bay, otherwise known as Bad Boy Lane.

The rest of the day I familiarized myself with the ESTHER. I called my girlfriend in Sitka, told her I was bringing her home a present. In the night lying in my bunk, I fell asleep having had a jillion thoughts about the future. In the morning, I woke to find quite a few people having morning coffee. I made myself a cup and roll a joint with the morning coffee crowd. We lingered in the morning, enjoying the Sawtooth Mountains, the blue of the sky, and the peaceful serenity of the bush. Walking back to the ESTHER, I noticed L.J. stirring around on his boat, so I said "Good morning." He looked back at me and said, "What a fucking night," as he cracked open a morning beer. I sat down on the bull rail, asked what the fuck happened now noticing the black eye.

"We went over to Rich's, started drinking that fucking rotgut" L.J. says. "He was waiting for me to pass out so he could fuck Princess. I wouldn't pass out, so he got mad and said I better hit him. I told him I didn't want to hit him. He said I better because he was going to hit me. So I stood up and hit him. Princess started to laugh so I turned around, let her have one and as I swung back around to look at Rich, he let me have one."

"Rich was still pissed because I won't pass out, so he decides to cook up a meal. He had a deer hanging. He went out and cut us off one of the back straps. He came back in and fries it up. Rich looked at us, says 'How was it, cause when I went out and carved it off the back of that deer, I took a shit and ran that back strap between the crack of my ass.' As he looked at us, he laughed."

"Sean, the Irishman came over about that time, all fucked up. Rich made everybody take their boots off and leave them on the steps so as not to drag in the muck from outdoors. Every time Rich opened the door to piss, he pissed in one of the Irishman's boots. When the Irishman had enough of the bullshit and rotgut, he opened the door, sat down to put his boots on, and shoved his foot in to a boot full of piss. It splashed back all over him. Rich was laughing so hard he couldn't even fight back, then the Irishman must of been drunk 'cause he put his other foot in the other boot - it was full of piss. Back at it they went."

I looked at L.J. and said "I didn't like that fucking guy from the start when Shiner introduced me."

L.J. immediately stood up for Rich. "He's alright, that's just how he is."

"I don't give a fuck, it's not how I am."

We started talking about me having a boat and L.J. having a hand crank permit. He said if I set the gurdies up, he would go with me with his permit. I took a set of hydraulic gurdies, turned them into hand gurdies. It took me a few days and with L.J.'s support, I was soon ready for my maiden voyage. Now that we had a viable plan, the scow floated us some beer. That afternoon, L.J. springs the option of taking Rich to crank the gurdies. "All he wants is a half rack of beer and a carton of smokes," L.J. said, "it'll be worth it." Once again I voiced my dislike for the guy. L.J. was persistent so I broke down and agreed.

In the morning, we grouped up, fired the boat up. I once again tell L.J. he better just do his job. We cut loose. L.J., being the veteran and

permit holder, takes command of the ESTHER. I
went out back to get the gear ready. We headed
into a little cove called Graveyard Cove. It is more
of a small 20-fathom pocket just big enough for a
couple of trollers to fish. Luckily we were the only
ones there. Not knowing whether there would be
fish or not as catch rates had fallen since I was
with Paul, L.J. told me to drop the gear to 18 fathoms. As I put in the first line, the wires started
pulling and surging - the fish were getting on. I
hollered to L.J. that fish were getting on the starboard side wire. I went to the port and started
letting out the wire. It immediately started surging. I got it out and went in to find L.J. sitting
there with a beer and a smile on his face. I looked
at Rich and said, "When we get in that pit together
and I tell you to go, you crank. When I say stop,
you stop. That's all I want out of you." " Let's go,"
I said, looking at L.J. as I walked out the wheelhouse door.

Rich and I got into the pit, engaged the gurdie, when I told Rich to go. He started to crank.
Up came the gear, the first hook with no fish,
second hook fish on. I hollered, "Stop." The main
line stopped. I pulled the fish toward me, clubbed
it on the head, gaffed it, and slung it aboard. I hollered, "Go!" and the line immediately started
coming up. Next hook fish on, I hollered "Stop."
The main line stopped, I pulled the fish towards
me, clubbed it, stuck it with the gaff, slung it
aboard. It was like this voice-activated system.
The gear went up and down on just a word. As the
day went on, I started to like Rich quite a bit better. Not for his personality, but for his strength.
For him, it was like going to the weight room in the

penitentiary. By the end of the day, we had pulled over 100 Silver salmon. Hand crank heroes. As Rich cranked the last line in, I stacked the last hook on the boat. We walked in the wheelhouse. I looked at L.J. and said, "That mother fucker is like having a set of hydraulics." L.J. looked at me and laughed that L.J. laugh, "awh awh awh," "That's what we'll call him from now on, 'Hydro'." Well, it stuck for the many years he lived after that maiden voyage on the fishing vessel ESTHER. A lot of people only know him as "Hydro". Hydro, no matter what kind of person he was, found and became a significant part of Port Alexander, Alaska.

9

THE OPPORTUNIST

I was hanging out in the back of the Pioneer Bar in Sitka. That was where the pool tables resided. Shooting the shit and some pool as well, I was doing a little drinking with a newfound friend of mine. He went by the name of Successful Sam. A tall scrappy kind of fellow, grease stained clothes with a little rust around the edges. We were bull-shitting along when Sam started to tell me about his grandfather's claim down in Prince of Wales Island. I've always wanted to find myself some "Alaskan gold". Boy, did he have my ear!! He went on telling me about how he knew gold was there. Grandpa had gone into the woods, found the proper sign. He staked the claim out, got it recorded legally. Grandpa was or got to be, too old to work the claim. He could find the coordinates if we could just get there (I realized this

meant me), which meant grub stake. This oc-
curred sometime in early summer. Whether I had
been trolling for salmon or longlining for halibut,
not really sure. There has been a lot of cocktails
between then and now. I still had a bit of cash left
in my pocket.

Sam went on, enticing me with more tales.
With something like gold or women I've always
been "weak willed and easily led." I'm sure Sam
had a bit of a handle on me. I was fresh to Alaska,
the young eager beaver ready for adventure, for-
tune and fame. Sam being born Alaskan, had
grown up seeing the Cheechakos come and go. It
was sort of like the whalebone handled brass bell
that hung over the center of the Pioneer Bar. "For
he who rings the bell in jest buys a drink for all the
rest." You help persuade others to ring the bell so
you can swill on them. Not to take advantage of
anyone, things can just get pretty scratchy in the
darkest hours of winter. It was easier to get a
drink out of a person than a burger. Sam had me
convinced. All that had to be done was to set
thoughts into motion. I was like a newly broke
horse being plow reined around. We packed our
knap sacks and headed for Alaska Airlines. We
purchased a couple of tickets to Ketchikan. Sam
had a sister there, a very shapely blond that I immediately wanted to dive into. She put us up at
her place. The only thing was someone else was
dipping their wick. Sam assured me that a cheechako like myself wouldn't be burning any midnight
oil, so I let it go; but each time I saw her I could
feel the flame start up in my loins. Of course, as
any prospector knows, sooner or later you have to
leave your thoughts of desire and focus on your

main gold, which will hopefully lead you back to the riches of luxury.

It was time to outfit. We headed downtown by way of the first bar we came to. We headed back to Sam's sisters by way of the last bar we fell out of. "There was always tomorrow," a saying some drunken philosopher came up with. Tomorrow came. I awoke on the living room floor feeling like death warmed over. The thing is I remembered was Sam's sister drinking a cup of coffee and looking at me from the kitchen table. She was looking so fucking beautiful, and I do mean beautiful, to me. I heard Sam roll over and wake up which concluded my little fantasy. We rolled up, got some coffee ourselves. All the while I was trying to take my eyes off what I knew I couldn't have.

Before too long, she took off for work. We started to conjure up another episode. I counted my cash, had less than yesterday. If we played our cards right, we still had our stake. Back down town we went. We were going to tighten up and fly right - just as soon as we stopped for a couple of beers to get even. And that's what we did. Then we actually found ourselves down at the local Army Navy store. We got a shovel, couple of gold pans, and various little items for survival. We weren't going to need much. The idea was to pack light so when we left we could move quickly. After all that, we definitely deserved to reward ourselves with a few drinks.

We're drinking and yakking it up. We decided there was one last thing we would need: a rifle. We still had time to make it down the street to the sporting goods store. Off we went. We decided to go with a .22 caliber long rifle. It would do the job for deer or squirrel. Plus, it was all I could afford. Figuring we would just run the grizzlies and wolves off with our mean looks, we packed the gear and the gun back to Sam's sisters.

We came up with the crazy idea that we needed to go back downtown to celebrate our upcoming "find." Once again, I awoke on Sam's sisters floor. Once again, feeling like shit. Except this time I didn't have two nickels to rub together. I never have figured out how a person wakes up with not even any change. If you get mugged or rolled by hookers, they more than likely are going to leave the change. But you know you've done this to yourself. I realized now my prospect for further involvement with Sam's family gold claim had come to an end. I was out of money. I grabbed up what gear that was mine, a gold pan and the .22 and told Sam goodbye. Sam was an understanding kind of guy. There was a big halibut party that the fish company put on. I felt I should shoot for that. Sam and I parted ways and I headed for the local pawnshop realizing that I had been a meal ticket. The pawnbroker offered me half of what I paid yesterday, which was just enough for a plane ticket back to Sitka and a couple of beers to get there on. On the plane I thought, "The closest I had come to gold was by the way of a local Ketchikan bar called the Gold Nugget Saloon." I learned you should always try to define someone's nickname before going and running off with them. Successful Sam. I should have got the hint right there. I just heard of a place where the gold is supposed to be boiling to top.

10

THE POETS

My Only Love Is the Ocean
Keep them coming
Or so they say
But what if I survive another day
And fools will have their gold
I might try to find a pile of treasure,
But the sea will take it from me,
It's heart of leather,
So the only thing I know to be true,
Theres something money just can't buy
In the big blue

By a fondly remembered Deckhand
(female)

Alaskan Crude

THE STORM
Listen ...
The wind was almost silent at first
So how could I have known that I'd be in
for the worst

Sure, I've seen gales and storms unending
the sea tossed and turned dementing
but this one was like no other
for it ripped at my soul like the loss of my
lover
Still I stool there steadfast at the helm
as each wave crashed at Neptune's realm
over and over and over again
a torrential sea with no end
slapped at me bitterly with her tail
as the rigging aloft bent to the winds wail
  down between each wave dark and dread

descending canyons with breaking mountains overhead
crashing and falling on my ship's tiny bed
still she would shudder and rise as the water did shed
I don't know how or how long I stood there
my white knuckles gripped the wheel
as each pounding and thrashing wave
would drive me down til I'd kneel

Alaskn Crude

"Oh My God" is my whispered prayer
as I wonder if there is someone up there
who cared
Because minutes turn to hours an days they
rush together
for when you're way the hell out here,
there is no escape from the weather
Where a man must search his soul
for the strength to endure
and hope that his courage is raw and it's
pure

But listen ....

Each ocean storm eventually ends
so this I dedicate to all of our friends
who went to the sea for the livelihood that
they earned
fought life's last bitter storm but never returned.

By Steve Little
F/V STONE LADY

153

Gift From Dan

My song starts
soft and sweet
singing and smiling with my friends
deck below our feet.

On an adventure I would begin
unaware
of the tragic end
on a freight mail boat.
I hitch a ride
not knowing I was the package
to be delivered to the other side.

Along the way with song and smile
we reach our destination,
we were waiting for all this while
with warm hearts amongst friends,
We were greeted on tie up command.

To Paradise: The sender called

One sunny, bright day
an over bushy dirt trail led the way,
Provided was a canoe
to take passage through.

With a gust, shift of weight, slide of hand
we lost control of our tiny command.
Now I struggle, now I fight, not wanting to
give in
Only to realize the journey was just to begin.

For a musician was needed so now I play
in the halls of Justice today.
Dawn rises, the sun sets and life is seeded
my journey has now been completed.
So look to every thing around you
know I abound you.
By Charlie L. Bower III

Charlie L. Bower III was born in Corpus Christie Texas, and later lived in Florida before heading to Alaska. He was born to a fishing heritage and became a third generation fisherman. He has made his living fishing the Atlantic and Pacific. He has participated in many types of fishing; long lining, trolling, trap, net, and dive fisheries. He currently lives in historic Sitka, Alaska.

9013838R0

Made in the USA
Charleston, SC
03 August 2011